THE BAD BREAK UP

BOOK FOR MEN

Heal Your Broken Heart, Bounce
Back After Failure, and Turn Your
Experience Into a Victory

BY: DAVID STEELE

TABLE OF CONTENTS

PREFACE

Your girlfriend has just broken up with you, as a result you feel awful, and I know how terrible it is for you. You feel dreadful and don't feel like living, and having lost your appetite for life, you don't see any sense in it. You have nothing to live for and have perhaps even suicidal thoughts. All you want now is to have her back at your side again, knowing that these are normal feelings in your case, that are accompanied by the loss of love and the closest person in the world that she had become. You may not believe that it had happened, and maybe it still does not get to you, because she was 'always' there by your side, and you were there with her always counting on her, and considered her a *sure* thing. Your love for her and her affection for you were not like others, it was something special, wonderful, the only one, you felt butterflies in your stomach, you felt so much in love, it was great to love and be loved, you shared your world, your sayings, yours memories, and common places.

However, I have to tell you that your problem is not an isolated one and everyone at some point in their life has to face similar difficulties and suffer their own. I know that it is a great suffering for you and a shock on a par with the death of someone close. Therefore, during this difficult period, you should definitely not be left alone. I went through it the same way and I felt just like you, maybe even worse. At night I couldn't sleep, during the day my stomach ached from stress and I couldn't find a place anywhere, I thought that I was going to go crazy! I was feeling bad, so bad that I needed a visit to a psychologist because I couldn't cope with it alone. I was looking for any help I could because I did not know what to do, and how to get her back; I felt that there was nothing I could do. We had been through a short breakup before, but we quickly got back together. This time I knew it was different and it was really over.

Did I suffer? Suffering, even to a small extent, does not begin to describe the pain I felt. I know what the pits are and I know what it feels like to be down and out, but I would not be writing this book today if it were not for the fact that I was going through it myself, and I was not able to make any changes to change it and help myself somehow. It was a long time ago and it seemed to me that it would never end. I will tell you what to do to suffer less and I will try to present you the whole situation from life and also from a psychological point of view, so that maybe by understanding certain mechanisms, you can make coping with this crisis situation much easier for yourself. Breakups aren't easy, but it really isn't the end of the world. No matter where you are in the world right now, there are people who are exactly in the same place, having gone through or are going through the same exactly as you, in the front line of fire, fighting alongside you in exactly the same battle. Here's a guide on how to pick yourself up after a breakup, rebuild yourself and your values, get up from your knees even stronger, and attract a new and better partner into your life, then fall in love and live on. You can call this knowledge a red or a blue pill. It's up to you whether you want to swallow the right one, the right one for you.

PART 1

FIRST AID

THE BEGINNING

Most of us don't want to be alone and everyone is looking for their other half. It is something normally encoded in a human being and everyone feels more or less the need to be with someone. After spending time together, being under the protective umbrella of a relationship, in the emotional comfort, convenience and safety zone, it is not easy to get used to the new situation and switch to other ways of thinking by learning to plan yourself, spending the day alone, and living only in your own context. The longer the relationship lasted, the longer it may take to get back on your feet. Unfortunately, there is no magic advice for this and better mood will come with time. There is a lot of truth in the old saying 'time passes and heals all wounds'. You have to accept that your thoughts will circulate strongly around her for the next few weeks. This period may be shorter if you really want to get back to life. It is normal for us to feel a great loss when we break up, the fear of loneliness, your self-confidence falls on the head, at first, the tears of sorrow come to the eyes of their own accord.

It cannot be stopped; you have to cry if you need to. However, it is actually a very important period that forces us to act, work on ourselves and develop. Unfortunately, when we are in a relationship, in the emotional comfort zone (we are so good, comfortable, we do not want to change anything), the feeling of the need to work on ourselves is much limited than when we are alone. People prefer old torn 'slippers', with holes in them, often already uncomfortable, than the ones you have dreamed about but are still unproven. That is why they are stuck in well-established patterns. Change always brings with it a feeling of discomfort. People hate being alone so much that they prefer mediocrity, even a trashy relationship, as long as they have some points of reference, so that they can hang their attention on and get this attention from someone. These days love means that people hang on to each other ineffectively trying to fill their emptiness and their shortcomings and hunger i.e. acceptance and interest, the sense of being important etc. and relationships based on such foundations, although from the side they sometimes seem like love, sometimes 'difficult love', sometimes 'great love', in reality they are not in love at all. It is more a contract of two people to fulfill each other's needs than true mature love. This experience can change your life for the better. You need to suffer yours; maybe this is what you need in your life now in the perspective of your entire future life. You're smarter already. Almost everyone in life has to go through something like this.

My world collapsed with a bang

"Understand that every 10 seconds on this globe, what happens to you is happening to others"

- El Loco

The break up could have happened suddenly, and the news about it could hit you out of the blue. I'd ignored the warning signals that the girl had given me during my first break up which I experienced most painfully, because it is not the case that a girl makes such a decision from one day to the next. Something must have been going wrong in the relationship for a long time, but it also hit me painfully like a collision with a runaway train. I took her so much for granted. The feeling of being completely surprised by a given event shows how improbable it seemed. We did not consider the possibility of its occurrence at all, yet, all relationships are for a time. It is possible that we would not be so shocked if we took a moment to consider the likelihood of it occurring. Nobody is distracted by the fact that it snows in winter because everyone expects it. We have lost a loved one, but isn't such a loss normal in human life?

You are not the first to experience this, and definitely not the last. The reason is that 100, 200, even 1000 years ago, people had the same problems as we do today! People fell in love, parted, broke their hearts, cheated, met, got married, staged weddings, had sex, were jealous, cried, laughed, divorced, raised children, lost their fortunes, and earned their fortunes. That will be so in exactly 100 years time. We are the same, only the scenery has changed. Nothing lasts forever, *nothing* at all! The things we become attached to come and go. Each relationship is time restricted. Because since when were you supposed to have a trouble-free existence? Nobody has given you any guarantees. As Clint Eastwood said, "If you want a guarantee, buy a toaster." Everything changes, nothing lasts forever, and each thing constantly changes. The problem is people think something is forever. 'My boyfriend', 'my girlfriend', 'my husband', 'my wife' - unfortunately, but all of them were only loaned to us for a short period of time in our lives. Perhaps to learn something and move on because each relationship is for a time. Each one of them! Sooner or later, whether it ends with the painful death of one or the other person, or comes with death in old age, the wife as the first or the husband. People come and then they are gone, and everyone goes their own way, because that's life, and knowing that, maybe it will be easier for us.

People take too many things for granted and are therefore not at all ready for changes or unexpected events. Remind yourself that these dear people do not belong to you (unless we are talking about slavery) and are given to you only at this moment, not for eternity. This is the reality, no matter how strong your affection for someone is. Enjoy what you have right now as it can be taken from you very quickly. Sooner or later, everyone finds out about it in their lives.

Don't blame her because your time together is simply over. We are all couples only temporarily...

SEVERE WITHDRAWAL SYMPTOMS

"-Why should I drop my past? Not all of it is bad.

-The past is to be dropped not because it is bad but because it is dead."

- Anthony de Mello

She is your heroin that destroys you, even though you love her so much. You have to find enough strength to say, "Enough of this shit" and do it. It is a struggle to return to a quick recovery! Showing the willpower to move on with our lives when our brain is trying hard to get bogged down in the depths of the past is a struggle. Your thinking, habits and behaviour are designed to keep your pain from not going away. You're missing the drugs. Dismissing romantic love activates the same brain mechanisms that are activated when addicts withdraw from substances like heroin. You show all the signs of addiction because what you feel is mainly addiction to the other person. You long to get the drug back and feel it good again. As with every addiction, there comes a point where access to the drug is denied, then it starts to hurt more than ever. It's like a completely drunk guy who thinks everything is fine and just keeps pouring even more alcohol into himself without realizing it. You are now like a drug addict going to the dealer "please give me a dose, I'll do anything so can just give it to me!" You don't know what to do. You begged, you cried, you apologized, and maybe you drove to her house and made a complete idiot of yourself. Tirelessly you search for the tiniest sign of hope. In the end, the girl loses all of her respect towards you and does not want to have anything to do with you too. Then we are gone, and for her we completely cease to exist. So we can try literally anything to get back the (drug), the feeling of the person we love.

She is now for you, as for Gollum, the One Ring. You have to free yourself from her completely. You have withdrawal syndromes, and each of her messages, every contact with her, every look at her photos is like taking another dose - in a way it helps (unpleasant ailments disappear), but it does not completely heal and the addiction persists.

It's time to take treatment, cut off any contact and abide by this resolution and work on yourself to become attractive. Put the drug down. For those addicted to sweets, it's hard to fight in the candy store.

MASTER YOUR IMPULSES

"Don't believe everything you think. Thoughts are just that, thoughts."

\- Buddha

Human nature is perverse. People follow what has become unattainable for them, and what escapes from them is inaccessible. Then they assume a higher value of something. Your ex-partner pushed you away, that's why you started to go after her. You see her go away and you try to run after her and stop her. This is your difficulty when you value too much what you 'lose' without knowing fully what you can gain. You feel a loss, and it is normal to want to save a state in which you are not alone. After some time, being with someone becomes normal. It's the sadness, fear, lowered self-esteem, the belief that no one will be found. You think to yourself that you have to fight for her because you will lose her forever. She's gone anyway.

"But I love her" – you say. Believe me that each of us loved, but by some strange coincidence, each of us loves them even more when they leave us behind, and when they come and say they do not want to be with us anymore, suddenly our love reaches its apex. It's the strange truth, isn't it?

Our brain is not such a good advisor as we think. You just *cannot* trust it. The deer's brain tells her to run when she feels that she may be in trouble, she gives in to emotions, impulses, bad advisors and runs ... straight into the street. Many of our behaviors, which tell us something in our heads, mean that we only prolong our pain, delaying the recovery process, and even in the long run cause problems with mental health or alcoholism.

Lots of people feel panicked after long relationships because they don't remember what it's like to be alone anymore and they are terrified of it. Many people derive their sense of value and attractiveness from being with someone as if you, as an independent entity, had no raison d'être. Someone who builds self-esteem in a relationship, becomes addicted to their partner, loses themselves and junks their partner.

What are you going to do now? At this stage you are not sure what will happen next. This is normal. You want to go crazy. As long as you are tormented by emotions, you are panicked and there is nothing you can do, because everything you do now in this state will not help you. Emotions play the first fiddle in you. You know the old project has already ended, but you're not sure what to do with your life now. Simply wait. A breakup is a sign of development that you might mistakenly consider a sign of failure. Remember that even though you don't have a girlfriend now, you have always been, and will be valuable, unconditionally.

IT'S HARD TO SWALLOW, BUT I ACCEPT IT

"*Pain* is inevitable. *Suffering* is optional."

-Haruki Murakami

She doesn't want to be with you anymore and you have to accept that. What, are you're going to be moaning like some woman now? Give me my girlfriend back. Give me back my toys? You have to accept that's it is a living human being and if you love this person, you should want her to be happy. But maybe your definition of love is to love this being only if it provides you with the drug in the form of sex, falling in love, intimacy, etc. Don't allow yourself to accept the fact that she now wants to deliver this drug to someone else or be alone. It is not her duty; her duty is to go in a direction that makes her happy and attractive to her. We are so selfish that none of us think of it that way.

If you really loved your ex-girlfriend, why not let her find what she wants, and not just what you want? It's her. Could it be selfishness and not love? Huh? If you loved her, wouldn't you let her have Happiness with a capital 'H'? To love so that the need to have a woman is not inscribed in this love. To love so that at the moment when a woman decides to leave, you can calmly say: "if you need it to be happier - go, and I sincerely wish you this happiness".

You can't help it. Therefore, you need to forget about her. If something has broken, there is no point in fixing it, and for you it will be a much better thing to be with someone else who will really like you, love you and respect you for what you are. You meet a woman because you want to give her happiness, pleasure, moments of joy and unforgettable impressions. If she doesn't want to, you can't make anyone happy. Accepting the fact that the one you want no longer wants you is the base, the foundation of freeing yourself from those lousy, aching emotions.

What could be more futile and crazy than the creation of an internal resistance to something that already happened? When you bang your toe and then fight this pain, the pain seems even worse. But when you hit yourself and say fuck it. If it hurts, then it hurts, and that is fine! Suddenly it's as if the pain goes away. Surrender to what is because the pain caused by the loss of a loved one must be transformed through acceptance. Accept what you don't want to accept. Acceptance does not mean inaction; acceptance is true strength and maturity. Learning to accept what we cannot change it hard enough and imposing. Accept your pain, it will hurt less.

> When painful memories come to you, surrender to them and accept what is now and what you are feeling. Don't fight or push them away because you are in quicksand and fighting will only make the pain worse.

HOW NOT TO GO CRAZY - THE FIRST FEW WEEKS

"I must lose myself in action, lest I wither in despair."

- Alfred Lord Tennyson

Help at home. If you have your own house or apartment, there is *always* something to do there, so clean up, wash the cabinets, sew a button on, iron your shirts, clean and polish your shoes, clean the windows, clean the glass in the wall unit so that there are no stains. Wash the bathroom, clean the tiles, the sink from the top to bottom, and clean the floors. Look through wardrobes for clothes that are old or torn out - there could be at least 2-3 items. Think about what needs to be fixed and try to do it; and if you can't do it now, think about how to do it.

Call mates you haven't seen for a long time. Make an appointment with them. See if you can learn a language so that you can go somewhere in the summer. Plan something, write down what you need to do, and start putting it into action.

Go cycling or fishing. Go for a run or watch a comedy. Meet up with your buddies. Clean up the house. Wash the dishes; just do everything to take your mind off her. Do everything not to think of her. Renew neglected and valuable contacts or do something completely different. Stop living only for that piece of ass or you will die miserably. You have free time so chill out with your friends, play on the console, chat with your family, build submarine models, learn to cut and sew, read books, clean aquariums, etc.. Fill up your day so that you don't have time to feel sorry for yourself and reflect on your ex.

When you suffer, you should resist the temptation to sit down and brood over your sadness. A very sensible plan is to replace fruitless self-torment with exercise. With physical effort, you reduce the burden on the part of the brain where reflections and spiritual suffering are located. Another part of the brain directs the muscle effort so that your pain is broken down and relieved. Physical activity in this way triggers the release of endorphins, the happiness hormone.

In 3 months time, it will be over. Set yourself a time limit in your head. So you think that after 2 weeks things will get better. DON'T DELUDE YOURSELF, as there will be more shit than now, more than you think and more than you can even imagine and more than two people could ever imagine and describe. It will be terrible, believe me. But then go for a run somewhere instead of running back to her. Zero writing! Just focus on yourself and keep trying. You will break down more than once, so give yourself 3 months to be in a fucked up state.

I know, it seems oh so long, but you won't even notice it. The first weeks, then the first 2-3 months will be difficult. Then it somehow flies, and you gather yourself together, and you don't contact her in any way. Exercise patience, patience and one more time patience and of course no contact with her. In just a month or two, you can be a completely different person. If you learn to think right and do what you need to do, then you will be, - it's guaranteed. Each day works to your advantage. Over time, you will return to your memories less and less.

Over time, you slowly come to the point where you find emotional energy for life beyond a lost relationship.

We learn to love life and other people anew, and all attention is no longer directed only to what we have lost. Many of us have a hard time with this task. We are afraid that we are killing the memory of a lost person by learning to love life or other people anew. Above all, give yourself time. Treat it as if it is no longer in your life, as if something good happened to you, but you know that something even better will happen to you. Work on yourself! Be patient above all, and results will ultimately come.

A lot of people say that when you sleep with a few other girls, that feeling wears off, but I know it's too early for you and you don't feel up to it. You still send signals to those around you that you are unhappy, even if you are not aware of it. You probably have a little loathing of women now - you only care about this one, and you don't want to hear about any other, let alone some dating. Take care of other things. If it hurts, so be it. Wait a moment because you need this time.

Do not force yourself to look for a girl now, it will kill you. Don't get into new relationships. Meet people, go to the gym, play tennis or whatever. If you do not wait, you will not suffer, and you will only put off the pain that is to come. You have to endure yours and suffer what you have to. Do not seek consolation at all costs. Everything has its own rhythm.

NUTRITION: HOW TO SUPPORT MOOD AND MENTAL HEALTH

You should know that diet, the condition of our intestines and what we provide to our body is largely responsible for our well-being. You should relieve your nervous system and brain, after these last possibly sleepless nights and long lasting stress which constantly kept you company. If you don't take care of your mind and body that you won't have the willpower to do the work that need to be done to recover after painful breakup.

- **Junk food=depression.** Avoid food that might make your overwhelming feeling of sadness worse. You should avoid trash, processed food for at least for the nearest future. By the way, now is also the best time to change your eating habits to healthier ones, the ones which will serve you better. Avoid sugar, artificial sweeteners, alcohol, hydrogenated oils, fast food, trans fats, processed foods, soy souce. But do not allow yourself to go hungry, because that's when the worst moods get us. Good quality diet: Healthy fats like extra virgin olive oil cold pressed. Fatty fish rich in Omega-3s such as salmon, herring, mackerel, anchovies, sardines, tuna. Nuts such as walnuts, almonds, cashews, peanuts. Avocados. Fresh vegetables and fruits. If you want to be fully alive, you need to have the proper fuel.

- **Vitamin B-complex.** Our nervous system is strongly stimulated by every factor of stress and need vitamins from group B. Supplement for a period of min. 2 months.

- **Ashwagandha.** Its a unique plant that has been used for thousands of years, it has amazing tension and stress reducing properties for the nervous system. It has an antidepressant effect. It's used in states of exhaustion, anxiety, tension. That's why you will also need Ashwagandha which will help your organism adapt to stressful conditions, emotional failures and various toxic relationships. It's not addictive and has no side effects. It's completely natural. Usually one or two capsules a day is enough to feel the difference after some time.

- **Vitamine D3 (sun exposure).** Vitamin D is required for brain development and function. Vitamine D3 5000 IU (units) a day.

- **Probiotic supplement.** Probiotics are live good bacteria that provide health benefits generally by improving or restoring the gut flora. Gut microbiota's effect on mental health. The gut and brain are connected. These two organs are connected both physically and biochemically in a number of different ways. Basically, your gut microbes can help your body produce more serotonin and other good chemicals that effect your brain.

- **Cold-water cure.** Ice baths can greatly reduce your stress, anxiety, and depression. There is a lot of information about the benefits of cold baths/showers. Some doctors believe that swimming in cold water has healing effects on the human psyche. Ever since the ancient times, they have been appreciated for their countless health benefits. Cold water treatment has a positive effect on physical and mental health. It soothes depression and improves your mood. It lowers stress levels. Icy baths give us a greater confidence and growth of faith in our own capabilities, as it is associated with overcoming fear. Look online for the *Wim Hoff Method* (The Ice Man) it can help you a lot! Start with regular cold showers every day for 30 days. At the start you can alternate cold and warm water. You will see how much better you will feel physically and emotionally.

WIPE YOUR NOSE

"Self Pity -- I never saw a wild thing sorry for itself. A bird will fall frozen dead from a bough, without ever having felt sorry for itself."

- D.H. Lawrence'a

You can cry at home. You can howl and I know you will, especially at the beginning, but on the street you may sport a smile on your face. You are ironed, washed, shaved and straightened up. In 3 months time, it will be over. Set yourself a time and exercise your muscles. However, protect yourself at the gym, because if your head is distracted, you can break something. Exercise and do it a lot (but with common sense!) In 3 months you can easily lose or gain 6 or 7 kg in your muscles. I don't know when you are reading this, maybe it's still winter now, spring will start in March and you will be ready for something new.

Get out to the people. Sit down and relax somewhere. If you ever wanted to, buy some nice shoes or a shirt. Relax and get a massage. Set yourself a cut-off date in your mind and then you will start to function normally. Do not behave as if you are „the one who suffered on the cross", as an image of suffering of all kinds. Do you think that if she saw you now in the state you are, it will make an impression on her? You would give her another excuse to run away from you even further. Be yourself, just the new you, and preferably look for something cool and most importantly, something new.

Let out all your emotions, do not hold anything inside. If you want, write to a trusted friend. Throw insults, piss yourself off, cry, howl, but never do it on the street. In the street, you must be smiling and upright, with your head held high. Be shaved, combed, and always wear clean clothes. Force yourself to smile before going out anywhere. Do it in front of the mirror, every time you leave the house.

BIGGEST MISTAKES WHILE BREAKING-UP

"The primary cause (of suffering) is innate ignorance and the resulting desire for things to be other than they are"

- The Tibetan Book of Dreams

Real life is different from the one in american movies or Disney fairy tales. These movies or animations usually end well and the efforts of the heroes are rewarded with happy endings. Unfortunately, this isn't the case in life. You have to behave differently than in the movies and not follow their example.

- Asking for return and a second chance. Nothing is more pathetic in the eyes of a woman, then when a guy begs for forgiveness. In order to break-up a girl has to have so much aversion towards a guy, to dump him and not have a guilty conscience about it. Otherwise, she would cry every night, because she's a woman and women are emotional beings. She has to gather enough confidence not to have any doubts about the break-up or getting back together. With your request, you put yourself in the position of an applicant for something, you show this by the "plead" method when you know that you are (at least in your opinion) inferior, so you try, plead because you feel that you will never get anything better...so you run with flowers etc. Apologizing with flowers will have exactly the same result here as thousands of other situations, so the opposite of the one intended. All of our pathetic moans are completely disregarded. We only confirm to her that we are not really what she - a woman - needs. How can we be? By breaking our dignity, we suffer even more, we deprive ourselves of our own respect, while getting absolutely nothing. Absolutely nothing. You are begging for feelings and women NEVER forgive that.

- Let's stay friends - let's be honest, you don't want to be her friend, you want to be her man. You don't need anymore friends. An undoubted advantage of such "friendship" is the pain relief it provides. It's like a type of morphine which eases the pain of a break-up. However, there is a very uncomfortable detail here. There is no relationship. You still love her, but you can't kiss or have sex with her and you don't have the possibility of forgetting about her. The girl is constantly on your mind. And you persist in lethargy for some time, until a new individual whom she begins to meet up with appears, and you stand with nothing because all this time you weren't doing anything, just waiting and living in hope that maybe if you persevere she will change her mind. This isn't the way! Very often an ex is keeping a former ex because he's a great tool of validation - nothing caresses an ego quite like an ex who can't come to terms with the loss of you. You have to consistently ignore it, you don't give a shit about her and that's that. Keep your honour, the doll doesn't want you - too bad, bye, find yourself some homies to hang out with instead of playing a girl friend for her.

YOUR ATTITUDE

Adulescentia est tempus discendi, sed nulla aetas sera est ad discendum.

Eng. "Your youth is the time for learning, but no age is too old for that."

If you cry because she has left you, how will you provide for her family? You cry when you don't have enough money for something? You are to be like the chief of the tribe! A crisis is approaching; you take a spear and go hunting to keep her safe, that her children live in abundance, that they do not lack anything. After all, women want support, they want good genes in a man. Do you think a crying dude will give her that? A guy who cannot cope with adversities? And what will happen when you get fired from your job? Will you break down? Why does she need someone like that? A woman needs a man to support her. She's supposed to take care of the house, and you should work your ass off and hunt for her and your children. Well Snap out of it. It's happened, she has gone. The worst thing is to panic and show her your behavior that you are a loser. DO NOT CRY! Don't beg, don't ask, as it won't do any good and don't apologize to her. Do you want to apologize to her for breaking up with you? Logical arguments do not work on her. It is influenced by natural instinct and emotions. Show her that you are a flesh-and-blood man after all; take it with your head held high. During the conversation, if she tells you that she wants to leave, respect that, and if you can smile, then do it. Say that her decision is difficult to swallow, but you respect it and accept it, and wish her the best, and no matter how strongly inside you are tearing your emotions, once you are alone, you can cry as much as you want if it helps, but not in front of her. If you are already humiliated and weakened, as I begged and asked for your time, then if it was a few days ago, write that you care, but you respect her decisions, etc. From now on, the hard road begins. The best you can do is stay silent, break the contact completely, and if you see each other treat her like a friend, without any sensitivity. If she calls, say you're busy. This break-up will give you a kick, but that kick is your hope for change. Maybe thanks to this you will decide to open a company, learn to play a new instrument, get interested in martial arts or take care of your appearance. (That's what you wanted!)

During this time, she can find someone, the so-called Comforter. The worst thing you can do is beat him up or throw him down or threaten him if you met her somewhere with some guy. Greet her politely, be confident, and above all prepare yourself mentally. When you meet somewhere at a party, come and exchange a few sentences and have a great time, don't look at her. Take care of other women, not for show, but because you really feel like it, and you didn't come here for her after all, but to have fun. You don't have to prove anything to her. She doesn't interest you anymore, and do not prove anything to her, your ex, friends or her parents. Do everything for yourself. Why do something for show, there is no need to do it, and there are other interesting exhibits that are worth spending time and energy on. You want to somehow 'play back' on for this? Why? Would a man do that? Come on, tell me? Doing something to get back at your *ex* is firstly a proof that she is still bothering you, secondly a show of weakness, and thirdly, a proof that even though you have become a more than average seducer, you still haven't found anything new since you have time to wade through the mud of the past like a little child in a puddle, I think it's time to grow up ...

The woman does not want a second 'pussy' in her surroundings. She just wants a guy, a man, a rock. Will you ease your pain by behaving in a manner unworthy of a man?

✳ GULF THEORY

The situation of being dumped by a girl has a lot to do with standing on a gulf. An abyss forms between the two of you, and you can't overcome it. It just is. The gulf is her decision. At this point, it's impossible to jump over the gap. She produced it, and she must begin to regret doing so. The difference between the two of you is that she is standing with her back to the chasm, while you face it and look at her. What do you think, how will a step forward end? When you start walking to her, what will happen to you? The only option is to fall into the abyss. You take one small step and fall. Then for her and for yourself you are forever lost. Possibly, out of remorse she decides to throw you a rope and gets you out. However, as soon as she judges that you have recovered she will throw you back into the chasm and you will be back in the same place. The moral of this is that steppin towards her, chasing her, bothering her only makes matters worse. You can shout to her, the gap isn't big enough for her not to hear you. The problem is that she doesn't want to hear you. Besides, when she is facing away from the gulf, she isn't looking back, she can't see you, yet she can still hear, for her it's a sign that you are still close and whenever she choses she can turn to see you, you, an abandoned poor mutt.

So what can be done in this situation? There is no other way, you have to turn your back on the gulf, don't look down, do not think about how to overcome it. On her side she will quickly find many positive aspects. Don't allow for your side to be a place of sadness and regret. Because on one hand you have a gulf, but on the other a huge space. It's time to move forward, walk away from the chasm with confident steps. Move forward. Arrange yourself over. I guarantee that there are tons of great girls, friends and opportunities on your side. Your side has many pluses, you can organize your time however you want, start going to the gym. Really, you can do anything! And never, ever look back. Go straight ahead, as far as possible. Zero looking over your shoulder, just forward.

At some point, your ex will come to the gulf out of curiosity, sooner or later she will be interested in what you are doing, how you're handling things, maybe she'll miss you. She last saw you when she created the chasm and you cried, apologized. How surprised will she be when you're not there. If that's not enough, she won't even be able to see you on the horizon.

Now there are three options:

She will start to shout loudly, calling you over to the gulf. If you come running right away she will think that you're still waiting just well tucked away somewhere. And she will turn again. And you, where will you be? Over the chasm again. That's why it's worth it to ignore her screams. Go even further so as not to hear them.

The second option is this. She comes to the gulf, she starts to shout, but she can see that the situation is hopeless, that you are gone, you arranged your life, you're managing, you've changed. She will then go crazy, but you cannot come back to the gulf under any circumstances. Live your life. She created the gap so she has to think about how to jump it. And even if it's a 100-metre long gulf, if she cares about you she will jump it without any problems, she will find a way. Then she will have to force her way through your side and you can slowly let her back into your world, where your rules prevail. This is your space, where you are a different man, tough, durable, richer in experiences and confident. Then you will yourself know, if you want to let her back into your world, or go for a walk with her towards the abyss, grab her by the collar and send her flying back to her side with one kick, creating an even greater gulf.

The third option is not very spectacular. She never comes to the chasm. She wasn't worthy of you.

No Contact

She must not exist to you. The quicker you understand this the better. Any interest in what she is doing is harmful to your mood. No contact. No fucking birthday's, no grandpa's death or brother's pregnancy - no reason. Do I offer my fucking condolences to my "former ex"? No!!! Because I don't give a fuck about her. I honestly don't care about her. You have to understand 0 contact. It's the only possible way out for you and your mental health. She can't see you, and you cannot see her. It will be easier to make changes. Believe me. The less contact, the calmer the mind and soul. Are you still trying to get her back? Then stop! It's the best, and sometimes the ONLY option. The less contact the better. Let go - you'll be healthier.

The fact that you will be seeing each other - is NOT good. Even via Facebook. Today, it is extremely easy to spy on someone. We have access to the internet, google, facebook or other platforms which can provide us with a lot of information in the form of text, photos or video. But, you must understand that every second devoted to tracking your ex on the internet, checking how she is causes you to feed your addiction and deepens the pain you feel. Do you want to break the addiction to your ex? Then you have to remove all traces of the addictive substance. One look at her new facebook photo, photos from parties, photos of her with some new guy can break you once more for another few days or a whole week. Deselect your ex so you don't follow her. Peeking at her photos, meeting with her - although it brings you temporary relief, it's like taking a painkiller for a tooth that has to be pulled out. Sooner or later the pain will come back.

Do you understand what zero is? Not 2%, not 5% or fucking birthday/Christmas Eve wishes. So you want to quit your addiction, but you still have her phone number, you follow her on facebook and instagram, and you keep your shared photos on your phone? What the hell do you need that for? You don't need her number. You think to yourself "I won't delete her number because if she calls me I won't know who is texting/calling me"- Do you have the number to your primary school janitor in your phone too? Because you want to know that it's him when he calls? No! You don't have to delete her from your facebook friends because that's childish, you set your profile up so that you stop obsessing her. You can set your instagram up so that you still follow her, but her activity (posts, photos, stories) are no longer displayed for you.

"But I'd like to know who she's meeting with and what she's doing"- It won't do you any good! She can even stand on her head and you won't care…Get it? You have to let the wound heal, but if you keep reopening it, peeking, sprinkling it with salt, there is no way it will get better.

You have 2 choices:

- You do not contact her, the chick comes back to you crying because you aren't chasing her - you win.

- You do not contact her, the chick doesn't come, you heal faster - you win.

In both scenarios - YOU WIN

If you keep in contact you're fucked; depression, alcohol, the inability to talk to a new girl, generally fucked.

JUST LIKE A SOLDIER ON THE WALL

"Don't be ashamed of needing help. You have a duty to fulfill just like a soldier on the wall of battle. So what if you are injured and can't climb up without another soldier's help?"

— *Marcus Aurelius, Meditations, 7.7*

The centre of the brain that is responsible for physical pain is the same one that is activated when we are rejected, which means rejection will hurt us just as much as a broken leg or physical pain. As with the physical situation, we go to the doctor to treat the wound, and here we look for help from others. You are seriously injured and you need help from other soldiers. As men, we like to think we can handle it all on our own. Do not close yourself in your own pain. Some people prefer to experience the alone and it may work for them. However, if you have such need to get support from family and friends, but you are afraid that they may not understand you, maybe they will laugh it off; they will not want to listen to it, or you do not want to admit that it hurts you and you are ashamed, etc., then try to get this support, find it, if not here, then with someone else. If someone makes fun of it, it means that he is not a real man and has never experienced it in his life. Now you have to go through it in order to become such a man. It's best if you have such an opportunity in order to start living in an environment of a loving family (parents, siblings, cousins, etc.) and friends, close acquaintances, and female friends, or professional help. Don't think its unmanly to ask for support. You'll get out of this sooner.

Your friend tells you to meet with him, or go somewhere with him or other friends, and you say, "I'm not feeling well, I'm not in shape, I prefer to stay at home." What should you do then? You should go out, then you can say later that you had a great time, but when you got home you started to think about her again, but for those few hours your mind was distracted and it helped you. Try to renew or rediscover the life you had before your relationship. You have to reactivate your new life as a single. Before you broke up, you were single and maybe it was a few years ago, but you were single and somehow you were doing well. You may be alright now, and you have to like being single for a while and stand on your own two feet. You will understand that you can have a good life being single, even if you don't want to be single right now.

> You don't have to deal with everything yourself, if you need help my friend, just ask. The more support you can get, the faster you will recover.

THE REASON SHE BROKE UP

The name changes but the problems remain the same because they are within us. That is why it is so important to delve into yourself sometimes, not to escape from yourself to the TV, internet, entertainment, parties, alcohol, but to think about yourself. The starting point must be a genuine, complete understanding of the mistakes that have been made, and the faults that must be dealt with. It is about being fully aware of her shortcomings, but it is primarily the awareness of *your own* faults that allows you to really understand yourself. There are various women around, and I do not absolve her from anything, but most of all, not seeing fault on your side for the same mistakes committed over and over again will mean that there be no positives from breakups and subsequent relationships. It is worth taking a look at why it is happening this way and not differently, and it's damn hard to get a reasonable view when our emotions are raging. Then we are very susceptible to all suggestions, and the patch on the burning wound in the form of an answer to the '*why?*'

question becomes a priceless commodity. So much that we are able to find the answer anywhere and match each answer, because each seems to fit. Sometimes, in fact, It's not anybody's fault, and nobody is really to blame, and the one who first realizes that falling in love is one thing and mature love is another then goes away. Nurturing the hatred of the 'mean bitch' is not the most effective technique. Therefore, it is certainly easier to say "I fucked it up!", *but,* on the other hand, you must not force yourself to look for great guilt and wearing sackcloth. Of course, if you do not draw any conclusions from the mistakes you made in the previous relationship; if after analyzing what you were, you do not diagnose what you did wrong, and if you tire your next girlfriend of being a pathetic sucker, after the first stage of fascination, she will also ditch you. On the other hand, if you eliminate the mistakes that you know that you have committed so far in previous relationships, your relationship with your new partner will be better than with the previous one. There is no perfect recipe for success, but there are many effective methods to minimize the possibility of failure.

- She wasn't the one

It's not even the fact that she left because we screwed it up. She left because we *didn't pick up and read the signals* she was sending us in time. It is very likely that she only left because *we didn't have capability to leave her in time*. Maybe you also felt that this relationship did not satisfy you anymore, but the woman turned out to be stronger to end a relationship that had no future. If that wasn't that, she left because we were too weak to leave. If, after 2-3 years, there is no 'engagement' the woman is bored, and if the guy didn't do it, it means *clearly* that it wasn't *what* he really cared about! The subconscious mind and instinct guides it. And usually the subconscious mind is *always* right. One of the main skills in life is the ability to give up *in time* from investments that do not bring any promise for the future. Maybe you didn't screw up; it just wasn't a lifetime relationship? Maybe the relationship wasn't giving any of you satisfaction recently, so the girl made a great decision. We part with our current partner in order to give everyone a chance to find the better matching half of the apple.

- Someone else came along.

A woman can be with a man *out of habit* only and exclusively. It is very difficult for women to get through life alone, so they even marry losers, out of boredom, out of fear, that they are alone, out of habit, and through lack of choice. However, as soon as someone appears on the horizon, they *get a kick up the back side* as many of them do. Such a man is a "temporary option" until finding a 'better' or 'final' option.

- The Man has become a lame duck

When we look at a couple who got married or started to be together very early and young, we often see that they judge themselves by their core values in life at the age of 19-20. There is a Martha she is one of the coolest girls in school and there is her boyfriend Michael. He is a promising, confident, well-liked athlete. However, after a while of being in a relationship with Martha, Michael plunged into stagnation. He doesn't go on with his life or career. When Martha got ahead in life and worked to become a doctor, she finished her studies and pursued her plans persistently. By the age of 25, there was no longer any great value link between them. When they were both 19, their common values made them a good match, but Michael turned out to be fucking loser and a lame duck. Most often it can be predicted that a marriage ends when the status of the wife keep going up and the man stagnate or go down. One of the reasons might be that your life was limping in some aspect, but you have the opportunity to fix it for your own good.

Potential is what counts, not what you already have, because the woman will quickly see through you and turn you over. The smarter and more intelligent that she is, the easier she will see that you have the following:

- a car

- driving licence

- house or flat

- a job

- money

- all electronic devices and gadgets

etc.

But! For fuck sake

- My uncle gave me the car

- I passed my driving test 15 years ago

- I inherited the real estate from my grandmother

- My father got me a job

- My parents gave me money

- All the mod cons are on tick.

And if I am left alone, *and* sooner or later *you stay alone with your own problems*, it will all collapse!

Because everything is *not* yours, only what has been given, what has been offered to you, shared, lent, borrowed, and credited.

If you slipped up you as a man have to deal with it, and the woman *checks* how you behave *after a break up*, do you have the *potential* to deal with the difficult times. Not because you already have a car, driving licence, and the mod cons, because you only have it 'for a while', on tick.

A woman has to test us all the time, and she often does it unconsciously as she was designed by nature, because a woman shares a man's fate. The man is like the railway track from one city to another. There is a train on these tracks and these tracks are his fate. A woman getting married shares his fate i.e. where his train is going, what the purpose of his train is, and what the purpose of his life is. All this symbolizes his fate. Who will he become? Will he become the director of the company or the main leader of a project, or who? Does she want to get to point B? Not necessarily having a house, but the woman's certainty that you are striving for it. It's not necessarily working in a managerial position, sitting idle at work and watching your account balance grow, but the ability to *get* such a job, *or* to pursue your goal, whether you want to achieve something and are striving towards it. Women also consciously pay attention to the wealth of a guy. They just simply think about what their life will be like with this guy. If a guy can take care of himself, it somewhat guarantees the fact that you will be able to take care of both her and your future family. If you're a role model for her, a guide through her life, she'll think a hundred times before doing anything stupid. And even if it happens to her, she will know why she is with you and will come back. Do you know what went wrong in your previous relationships? Do you know how much your fault was in that? Think through, review it and that's all!

- Too much interference from parents

NEVER, NEVER!! You must not let your mum, dad, father-in-law, mother-in-law start interfering in your relationship. No way!!! Then there's the straight road to achieve the goal. This means, it collapses and the relationship breaks down. The in-laws never have anything to say, given the fact that they are not in-laws yet.

People break up for *countless* different reasons. People change and their approach to themselves and the world change, priorities change, needs, goals and everything else changes too. As a guy over 30, I can tell you that with full conviction that I change all the time.

IT'S ALL JUST TRAINING

"If you faint in the day of adversity, your strength is small" Proverbs, 24:10

Do you remember the movie *Devil's Advocate* in which Al Pacino stars and Keanu Reeves asks him, "Is this a test?" And he says, "Isn't everything in life a test?" Yes it is a test. The test of your character which is supposed to show what you're made of. The difficulties are your test, but only how you deal with them can show you and other people what level of awareness you have achieved and what level have you are at in life. When things are going well, anyone can pretend to be a great person. When things are getting tough it really shows who you are. When a woman leaves you, she checks how you will behave in such a situation and checks if you are strong enough to get through it with honour. Do you think crying and begging will help you? Is this what your honour is about? Perhaps you want to bribe her with a gift or with a bouquet of flowers? She sees your weakness and sees that you want to buy her with gifts, that you need her, because without her you don't exist. I'll tell you this much, it's not very attractive to her. Women are not attracted to weakness. It doesn't matter how you start, but how you finish. It doesn't matter what happens to us, but the important thing is what we do with this situation.

For men, strength is the rule, which means we have to be strong all the time. But for women it is the exception, which means they only sometimes have to be strong in a relationship, just enough to prevent a man from feeling permanently alone with the problems he will struggle with. The woman can only *come in* when you have a broken arm, problems at university or work, and when you are sick. You and only you as a man will have to face life. The woman is only there to help you when (metaphorically) you have returned injured from a buffalo hunt and put you back in working order so that you can hunt buffalo again.

After a break up a woman *checks* up on how you will behave, and whether you have the *potential* to deal with the difficult times, because in life someone can always 'graze your horns'.

Life is brutal and that's fine because it has to be.

DO NOT PROVOKE RANDOM MEETINGS

"A hawk, even if hungry, does not eat grain; a warrior, even if he hasn't eaten, sports a toothpick"

- Code of the Samurai

Do not provoke random meetings. Never write to her, never call her, under any circumstances, at most the only thing you can do is RESPOND. You are no longer in her life, she's made her decision. You are a man and you don't care anymore. You've become unavailable to her because that's what she chose. The exception is that you go to the same party, you meet her there, talk during the party for a while. Perhaps, you meet her in the supermarket, shoe shop, or on the bus or tram. There's nothing wrong with that, but remember that if you call ... you will be extremely poorly perceived, so it's better to leave some things until the mud is dry and falls off by itself. It makes no sense to clean a wet jacket, because there will only be bigger stains. Giving in to the temptation to write to your ex girlfriend shows only one thing i.e. that you have no balls! The decision is up to each of us, and remember, if you meet her under any circumstances, do not say how much you missed her, cried, and thought about her. Girls break up because guys get effeminate. When you write to your ex, you simply prove that you are such a crybaby, and a wimp. She does not need crybabies. Act normally if you meet her. If she greets you, do the same. You do not treat her as an enemy; remember that you were together, you had your moment together, now treat her like a friend.

She has to realize that you have your own life and you do not have to panic when it disappears.

> If you ever get the STUPID idea to text your ex, go for a run for a minimum of 10 minutes. Come back and chill out.

THE END OF THE RELATIONSHIP

"Accept whatever comes to you woven in the pattern of your destiny, for what could more aptly fit your needs?" –

Marcus Aurelius

"I don't give a fuck about her anymore!" Who are you kidding? In one moment you will be glad to be alone now, and in a moment you will be crying, and that's normal. Realize you are suffering. Accept that you are in pain. That you miss her and that you'd like her to get back together again. Be aware of it, but accept that you have lost it. Be a man. Get up and don't lose any more. You already know why the woman who left you was right, don't you? Because she wanted to survive, to have something special, and she would be lost with you without experiencing anything (just like it used to be with me and with others). How can you blame her for that? Let there be no resentment towards her. Be aware of the fact that you have lowered your guard, just like a boxer has to himself after losing a fight. It did not work out? Too bad! I know the truth hurts, and that truth gave me a bit of a thud in my time. The thing is, this thud was needed, but if you lie to yourself, you've already lost at the start.

Severe pain can be a great alarm clock. Don't take it as a failure, but as a positive sign that tells you to wake up. The hard road begins from now on. In the meantime, as with many, you will doubt it and call her, and what's worse, you will go to see her and hammer a nail into your coffin.

Each 'evil' is a lesson from life that we must learn and draw the right conclusions from. Otherwise, we will get it again, usually in an even more powerful version. This applies to business, health and personal 'mishaps'. When we get hit in the head from life, it is worth asking what lesson life, God, or another form of universal intelligence wants to teach us. If your girlfriend left you, learn the lessons from this and move on. Such a moment will come for everyone. You are not the first nor the last, and if someone has not already experienced it, they certainly will, as long as you draw conclusions, and do not keep repeating the mistakes, then everything is ok. What you learned while collecting the whips on your own buttocks is only yours and that is why it carries with it undeniable value as any painful life experience does. Here is the only lesson from it all: It is the only way to become hardened. It is never a waste of time and you should never think about it that way. Do not treat your time together as wasted, because it is a gross mistake. You have a lot of great moments for sure, so there is no need to pretend you don't.

Advice:

1. Stop tormenting yourself with this chick

2. Cut off any contact with her

3. Forcibly distract yourself from these matters whenever you think about it

4. Get over it

5. Learn from your current and previous movements and decisions

6. Work it over in your head, find the reason, and accept it

7. Learn your lesson (correct what you have to correct)

8. Shake it off quickly!

9. Meet someone else, even a more awesome chick

10. Fall in love

11. Live on

PART 2

HEAD FORMAT

REALITY FILTERS

„There is nothing either good or bad but thinking
makes it so"

- William Shakespeare

Everyone of us sees the world through our own eyes. Someone who says, "this was the love of my life" is telling the truth in a sense, because they shape their reality by giving things such value. Someone else will tell him, "stop talking shit because you're 18 and you have no idea if it was the love of your life or not", but at the moment he says it, this *is* the love of his life and as long as he lives with that conviction in his head, he won't open up to another woman and experience another love. We do not really see reality as it really is, and what we have before our eyes is its interpretation made by our brain. The world is as you think it is, so If you act as if this person is all your happiness and your only source of love and there is no other love in this world except for this person, stop it immediately, because such behaviour only guarantees yourself failure. If you don't want a new girlfriend and a new relationship, you won't have one. It is all in our heads. As you begin to think that you are sick and convince yourself you have some disease, you will eventually become ill. This is how our brain works. If you keep telling yourself that you love her and you will never get over it, that's what it will be like.

Whether this breakup was harmful to you or really something good, is up to you. For one person, a given situation may be positive but negative for another. The same situation is perceived by two people and will be completely different, therefore the perception of reality depends only and exclusively on ourselves. Our perception of reality can be a source of strength or weakness for us. How you explain the event to yourself will have a great impact on how this situation will actually affect you. Conscious interpretation of what has happened to you has such power that you can make even the greatest of traumas disappear. You can find some interpretation for every situation that can heal you even from such a difficult situation as the loss of a loved one. Psychiatrist Dr. Karn Menninger expresses this well in one of his quotes: "Attitudes are much more important than facts".

Try to look at the situation from a different angle and come to the right conclusion - in fact, this situation is in your favour. Our perception filters, the lens we choose to look through, is something we have total control over. Something you didn't want, happened to you and that's tough! What is easier to change: a past event, or maybe our belief about it? You cannot control what happened, but you can control what you think about the situation. "It happened and it is wrong" brings two aspects with it: "It happened" is a statement of reality, and "things are bad", is tinted by you.

On the one hand, we have a specific event (for example: break up)	-> and on the other, we have the meaning we have given it.

Focus on what you have and what you can do! Do not focus on what is lacking but on what you have and what you can do now. The doors which were closed before, or which you did not even notice, have now opened up before you. The law of concentration says that whatever you focus on grows. Energy flows where attention goes. What are you constantly focusing on? An ex-girlfriend! Wrong! You must focus on new women, new opportunities, new goals and what you can start doing now. The more you think about the things you want, the more sensitive you are and aware of the possibilities that will bring you closer to the goal you are thinking about. You put new filters on yourself. Start thinking about a red car and you will see that you suddenly start noticing all red cars on the street. Start thinking about how awesome it is now that you are free and no longer in a relationship and you will see that you will start to see the hundreds of possibilities that you were indifferent to. Think of yourself that you are attractive and how many nice women there are, and you will suddenly start to see it all, because the more you think about it, the more strength you give this feeling. So instead of constantly thinking about what she is doing, what she thinks and why she does what she is doing, find yourself some other interesting activity and devote your free time to it.

Change what you can, and ignore what you can't. We will not change the world, but we can change ourselves and our own attitude. Nothing needs to change except your attitude and everything will change. The right approach simplifies matters a lot. You have to change yourself, and the world around you will start to change. Remember, the world is as you think it is.

LOTS OF BEAUTIFUL PLUS POINTS

There are many beautiful plus points to this turn of events, which I recommend to repeat out loud in moments of doubt:

- you do not have a child (if you don't, add one point)

- you do not have joint loans (if so, add another point)

- several million women are waiting for you

- including many more valuable ones

- and freedom close to the heart of every real man

- which brings opportunities with it completely alien to men in relationships

- you are free, she freed up your time and your resources which you can spend on yourself and others

- also think that it is good that some things have become known now and not, for example, in a few years' time!

> Think about the future, not the past, in terms of "what will be" and not "what was".

NEGATIVE FEELINGS

"Negative feelings are in you, not in reality. So stop trying to change reality. That's crazy! Stop trying to change the other person. We spend all our time and energy trying to change external circumstances, trying to change our spouses, our bosses, our friends, our enemies, and everybody else. We don't have to change anything. Negative feelings are in you. No person on earth has the power to make you unhappy. There is no event on earth that has the power to disturb you or hurt you. No event, condition, situation, or person."

\- Anthony De Mello

Imagine a patient who goes to the doctor and says what he or she is suffering from.

The doctor responds:

-I understand what is wrong with you very well, but I will prescribe medicine for your neighbour.

-Thank you doctor. It will definitely help me a lot.

Absurd? We do the same now, we think how beautiful it would be if she changed, if she changed her mind, if she wanted to come back to me, if she said that she regrets that it happened and that she still loves me... We want someone else to change for our well-being so that our ex, our family and friends would change. The only person who needs to change is you, and you are the one who has to take the medicine. It's not your ex that is going to change, it's you! Neither can you say that someone has wasted your life, because life belongs to you and no one can waste it for you. Only you can waste it yourself.

Negative feelings are inside you, not outside, in the world. As long as someone thinks that the cause of their condition lies beyond them (and not within them), they feel justified in maintaining that feeling.

No one but yourself can make you happy or unhappy.

GET HER OFF THAT GODDAMN PEDESTAL

"What charmed you so much is in your head and not in your loved one or thing. Once you understand this, the spell will die under the blows of the sword of awareness."

-Anthony de Mello

Why do you forever think that the best alternative out of all these thousands of chicks is this one, who, out of boredom or sentiment, is refrained from speaking (or not)? You say, "I'm afraid I'll never love anyone that much again," or, "I'm worried that I won't meet the girl I understood so well anymore." Your fears are fully justified if you think and act as before. Therefore, you have a choice, either you will change something significantly (and in yourself!) or you will suffer. Pain is inevitable, but suffering is a choice. For now, you are sleeping with your "dream card" under your arm, instead of tearing it up, get fucked up with friends and forgetting. Stop humming wistful songs like a medieval troubadour, because it's not befitting for a guy.

One of the most common tendencies we have during heartbreak is to idealize the person who broke up with us. Our memories which the brain always idealizes, erases bad memories to clear ourselves from bad feeling... We only remember the good times, and we do not remember the bad times that also happened. Note that over time we erase bad memories and only the good ones remain. The brain strives to purify itself. We don't remember these bad things. Sometimes there is an alcoholic father in the family, when he dies, the child says he had problems but he was basically a good man. We don't want to remember bad things, that's why we only remember those cool moments with our ex-girlfriend. You imagine how special and wonderful she was and now she is gone. All this makes us experience our 'loss' even more painfully. The mind, at your own request, loops around playing "THE GREATES HITS WITH MY EX".

We inflate the magnitude of our loss in our eyes, and delay recovery. That's why it's a fight - a fight to accept what you don't want to accept. Catching yourself with those internal dialogues that make you suffer even more.

Get her off that goddamn pedestal! Stop idealizing her. Don't put the crown on her head and don't sit on the throne because this person does not exist. *"But, she was ..."* No! She wasn't. The fact that you still think she was different etc. is just your illusion. This is misinterpretation of reality. You think this is your great love that you cannot live without. This is just your illusion, a virus in your head that can be removed, but you just have to want to.

You yourself created a number of pluses for this woman, you labeled her the perfect lady and the first thing you have to do is understand that she is not holy! You even make yourself believe that this person has characteristics that are unique. You justify all its drawbacks. Moreover, you exaggerate the advantages. There are hundreds of girls like her. There are hundreds of women who somehow look good, have a nice appearance, love, try hard, and are intelligent. It really can be done. You bear this within you, you stifle this memory, an idealization that has very little to do with reality, because there are no irreplaceable people. It happened, it ended, to hell with it. The other thing is to minimize the advantages and whetting the disadvantages. Try to think about her shortcomings i.e.

pimples, crooked legs, whining, etc. To put it simply, look for reasons why it is not worth being with her.

It all started a dozen or so years ago, when guys, due to mass hypnosis, the press, media, television, series, movies, male and female friends, set patterns, conventional thinking, religion and all shit related to social programming, put women on a pedestal.

Why do you care? What had she done to make her 'special'? Maybe she has got three tits? Or maybe she kisses wonderfully? Or maybe she wants to bring a dowry for marriage? Show me this uniqueness. She is of flesh and bones. She goes to the toilet, poops, and farts. *What*?!! Girls fart?? You thought her farts smelled like a botanical garden? Give her two days without deodorant and she'll smell like hell. She's not some fucking unique Ming Dynasty vase and she is no goddess. This is an ordinary girl, unique like any other, which makes her uniqueness ordinary. List *all* her faults, *everything* you know!!! Physical aspects, character, companionship, behaviour - everything! Secondly, stop seeing women as other beings sent to us to worship them. They are also people.

Once upon a time there was an episode in a series where a couple moved to New York for the first time, and went for a pizza which they thought was extremely tasty. The best pizza they'd ever eaten. Really delicious! But when they wanted to go to that place again, they could not longer find it. For years, they hoped that they would find it someday and during that time they idealized the taste of this pizza in their memories. One fine day by chance, they came across the same place where they were on their first day in New York ... The pizza turned out to be completely average.

There are thousands of amazing women, but for now you do not see them - you have tunnel vision. If it's not this one, it's the next one.

SEEING THINGS AS THEY REALLY ARE

"Don't weep for your sins. Why weep for sins that you committed when you were asleep? Are you going to cry because of what you did in your hypnotized state?"

- Anthony De Mello

"But I fucked it up!" You think to yourself.

Stop feeling sorry for yourself and making a victim of yourself. You did everything that seemed best to your knowledge at the time. You have gained valuable experience. Some of them have cost you a lot, so value them all the more. A real guy should take a failure on his chest, draw conclusions, correct what needs to be corrected and move forward without looking back at himself or at others. Failure is there to draw something out of, digest and shit on, even if it was a fucking spicy jalapeño and it's gonna be hell again.

Did you ever do anything stupid in the past that you were ashamed of? It tough, but everyone did something like that. Each of us once made a fool of ourselves when we broke up, humiliated ourselves, made a complete fool of ourselves, and lost the rest of our respect. This is the normal pattern that many men have to live through - first it's lovely, beautiful, normal and finally it's a kick in the ass. Then there are all the stages of self-destruction and decay that have to be passed through, like childhood diseases. Forget about it because nobody is perfect. The person who did those things no longer exists. You are not the man you used to be anymore. Why? Because today you'd not do that, you have the experience. Now you are someone else, so stop torturing yourself. Just keep on living and discard all regrets and negative aspects. Man learns all his life and dies stupid. Mistakes and errors are inevitable. They are part of evolution. It is not only inevitable, but necessary. No good things come without mistakes and tough experiences. I understand your helplessness and your pain. I really do! I have been there myself, but when a person falls, you have to get up and move on. We are only humans with our flaws, weaknesses, but most of all the strength to achieve what we want. The feature of a successful person is not that he does not fall, but that he rises again. If you need to, forgive yourself, forgive her, and go on. You have to forgive your ex-partner if she broke up with you, because this feeling of regret, anger, maybe hatred, primarily destroys the inside of the host carrier himself. These are very bad feelings that will poison you in the long run. It is not just about exempting someone from guilt, it is about making you free. Until you forgive, evil will not be redeemed and therefore will remain evil. About two thousand years ago, before entering the temple of forgiveness the great magician said "forgiveness is a gift I will make for myself ..." So learn from the lesson you have learned. Accept failure and learn from it and draw from it the determination to rebuild yourself internally stronger than before.

A man has to fail so that he knows that he must not foul and humiliate himself again. Everyone must and should go through it. The sooner the better. So do not regret what happened, just draw conclusions and go forward. You're the smarter for it already.

WHY YOU MISS HER AND THINK ABOUT GOING BACK TO HER

Maybe you want her back because she was the only woman who wanted you and who it worked out with? Maybe what you feel for her is not love, but rather the fear that someone else will fuck her from now on, the fear of being left alone, and most importantly, the fear that you will not rebuild what you had in common with any other. If you only want to come back to her because you are afraid to face the world alone, she will feel your weakness and will want to break up with you once and for all. If you feel like you want her back just because you're too scared and lazy to go out and find a new girlfriend, then you should probably stand in front of the mirror and tell yourself the truth in the eyes. Most guys want their girlfriend back because they are too cowardly, scared and lazy to go out, do something with themselves, go through the series of rejections that are a normal part of the game and find someone new. By doing this, you make her someone responsible for your happiness, that is, you give power over your happiness to another person. You tell her "I don't want to be responsible for my own happiness. Please come back to me and be my beloved again and the god of my happiness." Giving responsibility for your happiness to someone else is the worst thing you can do. Is she not only responsible for her own happiness and life, but now she must also take responsibility for yours? Would you like to take that responsibility? You gave your will and power over yourself to a woman, otherwise she would not be able to decide whether you are happy, depending on whether she is with you or not. You got addicted to her. Her presence in your life is a condition of happiness and well-being. How do you regain the power you gave her? You must completely *go forward* and just get over her in order to regain your strength.

Now you have to make yourself self-sufficient, learn to function on your own, or quickly find a replacement object. The first option is so cool that if you learn to function independently, you will minimize the chance of becoming addicted to another woman.

HOW NOT TO WORRY

"I wanted to change the world. But I have found that the only thing one can be sure of changing is oneself." - Aldous Huxley

Isn't that you focus only on her? Forgetting about other women? Oh, but you can't, because the Goddess would be offended or maybe you want to show that you are waiting for her, and she can meet, kiss, fuck others, live the whole life, and when one of them doesn't come out for her, she runs back to you.

Instead, you are wasting your life, wasting energy on lamentation, and she smiles at another man at the same time. The last sentence will probably hurt, but it has to, because in order to become resistant to certain things, it has to hurt first. I know you cared about it, but it doesn't mean that you have to poison your head with it all your life. When my friend broke up with his girlfriend with whom he had been going out for 4 years, he locked himself in his apartment. He was unshaven and unkempt. He said that he had completely lost interest in everything. What was his girlfriend doing at the time? She was partying here, there and everywhere. There were photos from Barcelona, Paris, and a trip to other city with her friends on Facebook. Has she thought about how much he is suffering? She didn't give a shit. She has already recovered from her ex. You think 'your' girlfriend is sitting at home and crying - really? Or maybe she's having a great time without you ... Your girlfriend is already being cured of you. She *doesn't give a damn* about you and your great love. While you are pouring out your sorrows, she's having a good time with another guy, forgetting all about you. I know it makes your heart ache when you see your ex-girlfriend moving faster than you and as if she's been doing nothing about the breakup and the time with you. You can make yourself a victim, or, you can use that anger as fuel to rebuild you life. You should be fuelled with determination because it is the best way to buck up.

Move your head and back and don't be inferior to it. Man, get to grips! When will you finally understand that life kicks those in the butt who can't leave the past behind and think *forward*? This is firstly pathetic, secondly, in 95 cases out of 100, it is doomed to failure, and the third is damned impractical and unwise. As you continue to sit at the computer and think, how is it possible that you are no longer with *this miss*, the chosen one, or worse, maybe you will drink -> it's a fucked up road to nowhere.

If a woman ceases to fulfill my needs (her beauty, sex, emotional closeness), then her role in my life becomes *nothing*. If a woman refuses to meet my needs, which means that she has no role in my life, she becomes nobody for me. The woman is also not stupid and she strives to pursue her own needs and interests without worrying about my needs and interests. If it were otherwise, she would not have left you.

WHY YOU CAN'T FORGET ABOUT HER

Probably you feel a deficit in intercourse with women, therefore her value in your eyes is overstated. If you had a choice of three other attractive women at arm's length in your life, would you even care about this one? You might feel sorry, but you would soon fill your time with these others! You keep thinking about her because you don't have any other alternatives right now and you turn this woman around like a dog at an old bone shack. One that has no taste, no marrow, basically nothing, but with no other bone on the horizon, what is the dog doing? There's an old bone to chew, because it just happens to be this one. The lack of options leads to obsession.

What do you want a woman to give you? I expect warmth, sex and deeper understanding from a woman. You should know that this is not the last woman you will have to look after and who will love you. There is a huge number of chicks of all types of beauty, intelligence and temperament, but it is up to you what you want to take under your wing, and it's probably worth knowing the whole range of flavours before you decide on one. You will meet many more women in your life who you find special, so better have a plan prepared for these situations. You have probably fantasized more than once in a relationship about another woman you liked or a passing girl or a female friend. You were impressed by someone, but you couldn't do anything because you were in a relationship, or worse because you didn't believe in yourself. It's impossible that you don't like other women. The main thing that distinguishes her from others, apart from her looks and certain qualities to get used to, or considering that the 'other' may have these better traits, is the bond you have built with your ex-girlfriend, and the feeling of closeness and deeper understanding. However, when it comes to something with someone else, you will also be able to build it, if only you believe in yourself more! If you did it once, you can do it again.

Now you think there is nothing better than her that can happen to you, only because of the lack of experience and the 'market research' and 'all that addiction to your ex'. You know that you are (at least in your opinion) worse, so you try to lose all remaining dignity because you feel that you will not get anything better ... so you run along with flowers etc. expecting nothing in return. If you'd see her after six months or a year, you might get a crush again, but *much more* likely you would state, "Oh fuck! How stupid and ugly she is." Believe me! This happened with my ex 3 years ago, who I have had no contact with since then, and when I last saw her in some photos I said..."*God, she was hideous and I kissed her feet. Fuck me*". You will see that she is not as perfect as you thought and you'll thank God it didn't work out. Then the entire "myth" of the former woman will collapse, so don't be surprised, but you need to be patient and take your distance. The effects will not come after 2 weeks. Unfortunately, it usually takes longer.

Having fresh wounds, it is good to move forward relatively quickly, then in a short period of time we get a distance that allows us to look at things from a new perspective. Perhaps you are not worried about her at all, but that you have lost your comfortable sex partner. In this case, it should not be a big problem, as there are several hundred million women in the world, and quite a large group of them have sexual needs as much as us, and often more. How long has it been since you haven't been with her? In the time you've spent scheming, lamenting, and how to get anything else done with this girl, you'd already make a fortune for brothels if you're missing sex. Perhaps during that time you would have already met 30 other girls, and maybe three of whom would show you a pussy. Is this *really* the only chick in the setting that you can try to do something with? I don't think you live in a 12-person village in the middle of a forest.

You don't have to wait; you have to take care of your own life. Do you want to live in the past? Think about it.

RAISING ANCHOR

"Being defined by a vision of the future instead of the memories of the past"

– Dr. Joe Dizpenza

The longer the breakup lasts, over three, four or five months, and as long as we work on ourselves, we start to notice other women, we just want to fuck... We begin to move away from depression (even with the help of friends, family, or the psychotherapist). Nothing lasts forever (pain never lasts) and in order for something to exist forever, *we must keep it up*. Even the Olympic torch must be held constantly. Likewise, the car won't go if we don't put in any fuel. The toughest guy Tyson, Strongman won't go if he doesn't eat a proper, solid meal for 2-3 days. We always have to provide the fuel for the emotions of the relationship in order to keep a woman falling in love, to an emotional state. The same is for our pain. Even the most devastating emotions that come with this experience are impermanent. Time heals wounds, if you do not heal them, it means that you still cultivate these feelings in some way. Everything that disappears, disappears as these conditions disappear. When a relationship ends physically, it must also end mentally. If it is still going on in your head, then perhaps some unfinished business or hopes are continuously holding it up. If you have any unfinished business that needs to be closed, items left unclaimed, her items that you haven't returned or threw away, take these items out to avoid anchor and misunderstandings. You know what an *anchor* is that prevents you from going any further. You will suffer for much longer.

> Yesterday has gone, now it's today, there is only the future and the man looks to the future.

THE PROBLEM WITH THE 'IMAGE OF THE EX'

We guys have it well, girls have it much worse, the biological clock is ticking all the time, they do not get more beautiful, they have to look for all the time as long as they are young and pretty, and every year younger girls enter the market, which is competition for them. We guys do not have to hurry so our value grows all the time, we gather our life experiences, our scars, our market value grows, with time we get a better job, start our own business, there's more money, wisdom, etc. we are mature, that's why guys often choose younger partners, and women older partners. Life is running out and she is not getting younger. The guy matures and can become more attractive, but *not* the woman! Suddenly age comes! Then one morning after a disco they wake up, and here they are alone! There is no admirer, no one has even approached last night! Because there were younger ones, and even if she has a super shape, her face has betrayed her age, and guys prefer the prettier ones. In summary, a man is like wine and a woman is like milk, and don't be afraid of making mistakes! We guys don't need to rush so live in harmony with yourself, at your own pace, and do not let anyone else account for your decisions. If you are independent and feel responsible for yourself and you do not hurt anyone, it is only your business what your life looks like and what you want from it.

Women around 24+ want a guy around 30+ to:

- be stable

- have a job (yes, they are comfortable)

- feel safe (if they are going to create a longer relationship with you, not a one-night stand)

- know about sex and how to drive a woman crazy

There is an old proverb which states that if you want to see what your wife will ever be like, just take a look at the mother-in-law…. The truth is that *every* daughter is a faithful reflection of her mother. According to research carried out at psychological universities in the USA and UK, it was checked what daughters did not like and what the faults of their mothers were and what they would like to change in their mothers. These studies were repeated after 10 years, and after 20 years. Do you know what came out? Each became the same as their mother - an almost faithful copy. Behaviour, views on life, taking care of the body, behaviour towards her husband, taking care of the children, taking care of the house, etc. So, when you get to know a chick and you don't like her mother, well... I would advise you to be careful. The family home stays in our heads for years, and even if we want to get rid of it, it will be extremely hard. Basically, a woman will not change. Maybe she can 'hide' things for a while, but then it comes out of her. As you know a guy can change, but women can change only for a while...

Look at her mother. Take a good look and remember that at around 40 she will look very much like her mother. You can shape her a little, set her up, but when it comes to:

-behaviour,

-figure

-looking after the household

-healthcare

-cuisine

-diet

-looking after her husband

We cannot generalize and take it as 100% true, but if a woman had a mother at home who did not care about the house, she would also, highly likely, make similar mistakes. Be careful and observe what is happening in your loved one's family. If a woman loves to rule, it is probably because the mother has the decisive voice in the family home, and daddy is in the shadows.

Falling in love is a matter of emotion, and love is a matter of choice. You have to be very careful who you let into your adult life.

BUT I DON'T KNOW IF I'LL EVER MEET ANOTHER ONE LIKE HER

I understand…

There is still the haze in the city you live in half a century after Chernobyl… women have one tit and no pussy. Is that the case in your hometown too?

Wake up, Man – *DON'T WASTE TIME!*

As for waking up, you are already awake, but just still too comfortable to move your mind and backside. What happened yesterday is the past. What happened just minute ago is the past too, and the sooner you realize it, the better for you. Don't waste time! People will always fear the unknown, but waiting and doing nothing is now the worst of all options! This is the slowest and most painful way, and no matter how old you are or what you have experienced, there is always a good time to start all over again.

You'll find loads of others, and more importantly – they're the ones that are supposed to DESIRE meeting you. You're just supposed to choose whether you want to. There are over 6 billion people in the world, there must be someone there who fits better. There are women in this World also for you, woman who will appreciate what kind of man you are, and who understand the beauty of your thoughts. You will meet those who you want and if you strain your brain they will appear sooner or later. Your ex wasn't the only person on the planet who is capable of loving you.

There are a huge number of babes around, of all sorts and mystique, of beauty, intelligence, and temperament. Each loss is painful, but you should draw conclusions from every situation and learn from them. That's the way life is, and you need to change a little to choose wisely. She wasn't the one for you. You are still a seeker and you must understand this. It must hurt because the treatment of any addiction is painful. The treatment of the addiction of another person, or more precisely the treatment of a purely subjective ideal picture of 'the one and only', because that's what it's really about - the idealized picture - hurts most of all.

You lament like a mother who has lost her child. Since you were so special for that one, so you will be for the next one, believe me. Your asset will be that you will be wiser from this experience. You grow out of some things, and mature in others. There are certain women in life to discover what you don't want, and what you are looking for. They could be the woman for you at that time, but maybe you just grew up mentally, and in terms of your self-esteem. Now and for the rest of your life you have legs to stand on and if you screw up, you won't have legs to stand on for the rest of your life. People wouldn't divorce and marry someone else again if there was one love for the rest of their lives. Love is what you can imagine and build upon that which you are capable of. You still think that you won't love anyone else, because that's what *every* man in love who gets a kick in the ass thinks for even a moment. It's just like the one who vomits from boozing over the toilet swearing never to touch vodka ever again!

Are you sure you can't afford to meet a more interesting woman? Is this the peak of your aspirations? Come on!

THE FOUNDATIONS

Do you remember your pain? Make sure you understand that it is not getting about back on your knees to cure them.

You just delude yourself into believing that without her you won't be able to be happy. You are simply deceiving yourself into believing. These are just tricks of the programmed mind. Don't ask her questions. Whatever questions you ask her, you will always be disappointed. Your ex-partner doesn't know how to help you, how to deal with your grief. Even if you talk to each other in a friendly way, even if you remain on good terms, she will feel embarrassed that you still haven't come to terms with it and you are disturbing her normal life. It does not cure your pain at all. At the moment where you are so terribly frustrated between what your common sense tells you and what your emotions are telling you, you need to realize that you don't really want your ex back. First of all, you want *yourself back*. She took a few small blocks away from you but it ruined the entire structure, and now you think you need her. The thing is that you need the few building blocks she holds without even knowing it. It seems to you that the easiest way is to go back to your ex, but these blocks can be rebuilt in yourself and with even better material, but it takes time.

It is not the breakup that causes you pain or the cause of it; the breakup is only the result of what you have done with your life and *yourself*. There are no solid foundations of happiness that you carry within yourself and not built on a woman. It's not about your ex, it's about the illusory happiness that you think she gives you. As long as you are *not* an independent, self-sufficient being, you will be laying the foundation on a woman. Then the breakup is always a kind of your own death, because your whole world goes with the woman. If you accept the fact in yourself that people come and go, you remain emotionally independent as much as possible and do not derive self-esteem from your relationship with a girl, you will get through a possible breakup. The one who has no foundations in himself puts them outside, and this is simply unreasonable and extremely dangerous. This results in a lot of unpleasantness, and seduction failures are just the tip of the iceberg.

Ask yourself what you want in life. I guarantee that when you analyze this question you will answer: "I want a nice woman", but why? I will ask another question .., "because I want to have a good time", but why ...? "because I want to be happy". Is this woman the only way to be happy? This question is the most relevant. Can you do something to be happy and not necessarily be with this woman?

THE ONLY SOURCE OF YOUR HAPPINESS

You feel bad when that person leaves. You want her back. You only do it for yourself. You do it only because you are addicted to this person and you need that person to be happy. The problem is, you got addicted to this woman. Her presence in your life is a condition of happiness and well-being. No lady equals no happiness in your existence. This is a mistake equivalent to shooting yourself in the knee. If you had your life, she wouldn't take it away from you by leaving you. Apparently everything was under her thumb.

A woman cannot be our only happiness in life. If the relationship ends (and someone has no acquaintances or friends, no things they like to do or groups they like to spend time with, other people with whom they may have an emotional closeness) then it's a tragedy. Then that's just simply freaking out. The worst thing about a relationship is to end it, neglect it, and put old acquaintances and friendships aside. This is the biggest mistake you can make when entering a new relationship. The relationship ends and everything ends. Someone then not only loses their girlfriend, but their entire social life. You have to meet people all the time and that means new people. Or What? Your buddies go to seaside, there will be an accident and everyone in the car will die, and you will end up being alone?

A woman clings to a man who doesn't need her to be happy. It's about a man who has a life that he enjoys each day. Which woman will look at a guy who looks like a beaten dog? And he wants her to be happy because without her he will be unhappy, and she is the whole world to him. We are not here to make a woman *happy*, just as a woman is not here to make us happy. If you do not have these foundations within you, then you are prone to become *addictive* to a loved one.

Before you have a successful relationship with another person, you first need to have a successful relationship with yourself and love yourself. You must be happy with yourself first. You have to be happy first without women to have women. Go on a date with yourself. Fall in love first, get to know yourself. You need to be happy with yourself to pick up a great chick. You have to be open. If you do not feel comfortable when you are alone, or if you cannot love yourself, you will start looking for a new relationship in order to cover your shortcomings with it, after which the whole situation may repeat itself if you do not change what the world is trying to show you now.

If you try to pursue happiness only through a personal relationship and a girlfriend, you will face a series of disappointments, because you will be attempting to rediscover yourself externally, and then put right what you cannot provide for yourself i.e. self-esteem, unconditional self-acceptance and your own happiness. Only when you become happy with yourself will you be able to afford to have a nice chick who will be happy with yourself and only then will you be able to build a valuable relationship. If from the position of lacking in such, you enter into any relationship with any woman, or you build the whole meaning of life on this relationship, it will end sooner than it starts.

It doesn't work in the way that it's the woman and the relationship first, then self-esteem and meaning in life. It works the other way around: you take yourself by the head, and once you know what you would like, what you are going to do, what your value is and why it is so much, then it's time for a woman. Do not look for male and female salvation from the prickly life, because people with a shitty sense of the value of their shitty life only get shitty relationships, and there are very rarely exceptions to this rule. You can't say I want a girlfriend; I want someone then I'll feel happy. No! You must be happy, then you will have someone in your life. Gold attracts gold. If you are in need, it means you are not well. If you experience something lacking in your life, you will attract something lacking. Get to the point where you don't need her or any other woman.

You have to be happy regardless of her. The best thing you can do is show her that no matter what happens, you'll still be happy, with or without her. It's great with her ... without her it's okay too. You're automatically heading for happiness. It's incredibly powerful. She is not responsible for your happiness. You have confidence in your future, which makes guys incredibly attractive. You have to have an interesting life and be confident. Do you know what characterizes a valuable, attractive man? Make yourself happy yourself, then the lady will appear herself and she won't be the only one, and you will have a choice. Nobody really talks about it, but the woman doesn't want to be the most important thing in her man's life. She will feel that his happiness depends on her and thus will feel overwhelmed by his need to feel and cling to her. She wants her man to be fully committed to his highest purpose in life, and to love her fully, even though he will never admit it. If you do not live up to your inner self and offer your fullest gifts to the world, then everyone will feel you lack your true purpose. When a man is on his path, he needs nothing externally to be happy. Women are an addition to his life, he enjoys being with them, but he does not need them. Women complement the adventure of his life, not his main objective.

If you want your relationship to be the fulfillment of your life's path, you must first learn to be completely happy being single, and then choose to live with another person as a complement to your path, and if a woman has needs that are in total conflict with your mission, then you are with the wrong woman. One of the most important questions you can ask yourself is where am I going and who will go with me. If you ever ask yourself those questions in a wrong order you will have a trouble. What really attracts a woman is the realization that the life of the man she is with is not only a relationship with her. Don't put your former or current women at the centre of your world. Let them be part of it in the present or a memory, but never in the centre.

The basis [starting point] is first of all a change in the perception of your own person, because it will not win anyone's sympathy if you loathed yourself or constantly hated who and what you are, and what your life is like. It is impossible to love someone who is not happy with themselves. If you feel inner happiness, it is very easy for you to meet new people and acquire women, and they feel it when someone lives in harmony with themselves. Without this basis we do not have anything to say about the further levels of life ... It's extremely bad to enter into a relationship with the assumption that I'm not satisfied with my life and myself and I know it, but when I get into a relationship everything will change! Seeking salvation from your personal and huge problems is the worst possible solution.

Independence comes precisely from the fact that you are at peace with yourself, interesting and cool for yourself, you have goals and you carry them out. You are able to take care of yourself and spend time with yourself so interestingly that with almost a hint of regret you give away some of this priceless time to your mistress. You don't 'kill' the time you have for yourself, you are not waiting to meet someone because you live your amazing life. Then you have everything, and you are the champion of the world and the surrounding area in the eyes of the lady, and a king in your mysterious kingdom of self-happiness. It's simple because he who is not happy with himself will not bring happiness to anyone. If one side does not have their own life, they will always expect the other side to give up their life in the name of a great union. It doesn't work that way. Love is when two healthy, independent people meet. Then they do not hang on themselves, there is no pathology. For the other, one is a beautiful complement to life, not its content and necessary condition. Then no games are needed, because no one has to force the strength of the other's love, fight for domination and pull the strings.

Have your life and hobbies and don't live her life, because your only hobby will be herself, and that always ends in a tragedy. So that in the future the breakup, i.e. loss of one of the 50 spheres of life, does not deprive you of your testicles, head and everything else that is needed for this life.

Enter a relationship to improve your already great life, not to be your life. This is all about becoming a man who has such great life that he wants to be single first.

THE MENTAL LOOP

"You cannot get rid of a bad habit, you can only
replace it with another habit"

-Strength of Habit

Humans are lazy by nature. I do not mean that they would be most willing to sit on the couch at home all they, but rather they are mentally lazy, not taking the trouble of conscious thinking and too often thoughtlessly transferring power to emotions over reason. You will probably say that "it's independent of you" and I will tell you that you do not practice positive thinking. You are what you imagine you are. As long as you are, in your consciousness, a poor boy abandoned by a woman, you will be exactly that. Each thought is in the tone: "I feel a great emptiness, we were together so much time, it was so beautiful, we experienced so many beautiful moments between ourselves, two months ago we were on vacation together and she said that she loved me." It does not bring you a within a whisker of changing for the better. This is gloating over the past, so leave yourself such thought processes on the rocking chair when you are 90 years old. Cultivating such thought journeys is the first step to hell. Maybe you could do something else, without grinding many moments together before your eyes? Did you have your life, or if you took your nose out from under her armpit, you have nothing to breathe with? Each success is based on the same i.e. thinking forward, not backward, *believing* that it will work and it will get better. Everything begins with this faith and everything depends on it. Let this past serve you only to draw conclusions that will help you avoid mistakes in the future. In life those who rise too slowly from the ground lose. When you lie down and squeal, everything is happening next to you, and you are not participating in your own life here and now. This situation proves that your own life was too miserable, unrelated to a woman. If, for example, while in a relationship, you had to spend time for yourself to build a model of a medieval castle in a 1: 1 scale, cleaning the chain from the ship on which your great-grandfather used to sail, learning to juggle ten chainsaws, or breeding a murderer's guppy by crossbreeding, now you would go for it and you would have forgotten it long ago. You wouldn't have time to live in the past. Now you apparently have too much time, you have nothing to do, you do not have enough value for yourself, you do not find fulfillment in your own independent being, so you deal with suffering as a hobby. In addition, thinking "she rejected me" acts like a mantra and brings your sense of meaning and self-worth to zero. Take control of your mind and stop wasting time. This is a small steps technique, so forcefully distract your attention from intrusive thoughts whenever they arise - the first 100, 200, 300 times will be difficult, then it becomes a habit, and you will habitually think of something else.

For some it will be faster than for you, and for someone else it will go slower. Don't blame yourself for thinking about her. You will think about her for a long time, but in the end, the day will come when you will say to yourself, "I haven't thought about her for half a day." Soon there will come a day when you will realize, "Fuck, yesterday I didn't think about her at all". All the time, however, remember that thinking about her is a bad habit. Accept the thoughts about her, accept the pain because we are only human, but give yourself some mental discipline. Every time you find out that this cunt is in your head, put something else in there. There are dreams, tasks, and another girl. By force!!! It's your job. She will disappear from your head. Form, muscles, skills, and knowledge will remain. That is why it is so important to do something else.

THE WAY OF A MAN

A weak woman remains in this stagnation, she is afraid of what to do next, that she will not find anyone. A strong woman says, "that's it! I can do it alone".

It's the same for men.

How a guy sees the role of a woman in his life, how strong he is internally, and for which he needs a relationship with a woman. A woman's intuition classifies a guy as one who needs a woman in the wrong way, in a word - he is "needy" from the very beginning. A man who is prone to addiction to a woman, draws strength from the relationship, instead of himself, surrounds and limits women, for whom the relationship is the meaning and purpose of life, and not one of the areas, is a weak man. Anyone who does not have a well-built self, does not have solid foundations and internal, strong self-esteem, and sooner or later he bends with 'dependence', begins to hang on the woman and depends on *her*, and the woman feels it and the problem arises *here*.

A man should have a natural thrust for success, be ruthless when necessary [the situation demands it], and not deliberate over bullshit, or dwell on the sufferings and sorrows. In my opinion, a man has no right to expect his woman to feel sorry for him and join him in suffering. Why do you take away the girl's right to be weaker, because suddenly you wanted to be understanding for your pathetic ways? So who is ultimately to be the helmsman in the relationship? Everyone can cry, but it seems that for women we are supposed to be something more than a mental version of another woman, differing only physically, because the woman you are with is not your mother. Remind yourself that you are not meant to be a woman. You're supposed to be a man. A *fucking* man, unfortunately, who constantly has to decide, without any doubts. You have seven breaths to make a decision, as it is written in the samurai code. What about you? Do you leave things to the female who needs care? A guy? A man? You hand over power to her, push the decision onto her, so what is it? Are you too weak to make such a decision? How can she trust you? You are just supposed to possibly *let* her be with you, and if you don't, you will go away. They want to be weak, and they want a stronger one. They want to be directed. Understand that! She needs to see that the guy has a plan for himself and knows how to implement it easily and consistently. It's an idea for yourself. This one woman will never forgive guy: if he has no idea for himself. No plan for the future. If he goes blind without seeing any path, he makes this path from new every day. I don't mean to say that all women are the same. They most certainly are not. All I'm saying is that the rules of the game do not change, and on the captain's bridge, there is only room for one captain. No matter how vulnerable your dearest seems to you, and delightfully clumsy and cute, always remember, she wants to be one too. She wants to rule. The paradox is that when she finally takes over the helm, making you an effeminate lame, she ceases to like the fact that you are such an effeminate lame. And what? And, *boom*!!! *A kick in the ass*! Well, what does she need a man for who isn't even a man anymore?

A man's lead in a relationship is mainly based on the fact that you don't stand in front of a flour rack in a hypermarket until death. At some point, as a guy, you break this farce, you go to a fucking shelf, take some fucking flour, put it in a cart and gracefully go away, and then a wave of gratitude from the woman you saved from standing to death in front of that flour rack comes over you ;-)

Help me because she dumped me, what do I do, because I upset her and she left me - do I call her or not? Where is the male self-confidence and the attitude of a man who solves the problem on his own and does not run to his mother? I know where the fault lies. I guess some parents patted and puffed too much to make their son feel good. Perhaps they did not teach him enough duties and responsibility. Our mothers are often responsible for the effeminacy of men (with all due respect, who in their opinion want the best), as well as the effeminacy of the teaching profession, which definitely gives non-masculine models. At one time the teacher was such that it was frightening to squeak. At the moment, practically all ladies are sitting there, usually old maids. So how are they supposed to raise young guys? Well... oh, there are no fathers. It's work, or he doesn't feel like showing his manhood to his son. Another thing is that over the years we are instilled with some nonsense, and then we need a few years (if someone notices it) to unscrew how a man should actually behave, and because of his age, he should usually already be one for a good few years. Another clear symptom of a certain infantilism is simply and above all a mere lack of experience than attributing it to anything else.

Remember that subconsciously, a woman needs a partner who will guide her in life and that she will be able to count on his strength in the future. This is the sense of security. Go back to your childhood and think about how you felt with your parents, mainly about your father. Not everyone is lucky enough to grow up with the right role models. A friend of mine who is very grateful for the upbringing and attitude he received from his father put it like this: "I have never but never seen my father in a woeful state. He always found a way out of the situation. For us children and our mother, he was a support, just like our grandfather." "He taught us the principle that he asked only twice, and there was some punishment the third time round, e.g. the order to clean the room meant that if I didn't do it, I would find things beyond the window and I would have to pick them all up. On the other hand, he was very honest and fair. He did not punish unnecessarily and gave as much positive energy as he did punishments." "My father always said that when I grew up I would prepare my own fate and write my own biography." My grandfather was like that in my family. I knew that he would always get out of any trouble. I believed and knew that he would not break down and would not pretend that there was no problem, but that he would resolve it. He will do everything so that things are as they should be. This is self-confidence and strength of character, and it feels like it; but nobody was born a gladiator, they developed this inner strength by struggling with problems. To develop it, you must first of all get to know yourself and admit your weaknesses and fears to yourself, and then face them. Don't confuse self-confidence with being cunning or flash like most guys. Women don't want a partner who pretends to move mountains and no one will mess with him. Nobody is alpha and omega, so if we don't know or can't do something, it's necessary to admit it and try to change it. It's about self-confidence and believing in your own strength!! Women are there to scratch at every problem. You as the male species are there to solve problems or doubts, not to discuss them. How is a woman supposed to feel that you are strong or can trust you if you do not feel it yourself? More strength and self-confidence!! It will help! I won't mention honour. When you look in the mirror who do you see? A tough guy or a poser who pretends to be a tough guy and hides his fears of life. So don't confuse being tough with being the strongest as far as your mouth or muscles are concerned. I know many muscle men, bodyguards who only have shell on the outside and yolk inside, which spills out every time someone scratches the shell. Believe it or not, if someone is confident, if someone has a strong character, nothing will upset or offend them when you throw mud on their face. This is what the weak do who defend their own image. They defend it so that others can see this image intact. A tough man does not have to defend a lie.

Look at yourself and correct what you don't like. Do not look at others only at yourself, all the others won't feed you!

MAYBE SHE WILL COME BACK TO ME

You cannot create the illusion of imaginations. Blinded, you want to get only the answer that is your 'dream answer'. You are looking for the tiniest signs which mean that there is still hope. You remain in hope, in stupid hope, remembering the moments that have passed and will not come back again. Doesn't it irritate you? Aren't you fed up with this? Ignoring reality, drifting off into dreams, and pretending otherwise won't make things better. When are you ready to turn your illusions into reality? I would like to advise you that "it will all work out! It will be great; you can do it! I believe in you, and that you will be married."… => But that's not gonna fuckin' happen. That's the truth, unless you prefer sweet pink little lies. The disintegrating illusion hurts painfully. Everything you think you've built is starting to fall apart and that hurts. Reconcile with it and don't fight it. You must realize the fact that she will never get back to you, nor will you ever meet her again. You are right to assume that you will never be together again because she has gone forever. When you send her signals that you are waiting for her, she will think. "oh, he is waiting, I'm using my life. I will look for someone better and if I do not find anyone better, will I go back to him?" It's the perfect solution for her. Is it for you too? Do you want to be a reserve and wait for the scraps from the table? If she tells you "let's be friends", you already know what she wants to achieve. Don't get into it !! Although, you may think that it will keep you close to her, in fact you will be suffering literally and endlessly. You will be a plant that she will water from time to time, so that you can live for yourself and be her property, such a security that if something happens, you are there. Understand that! Don't wait, you have to take care of your own life! When you live your life completely accepting what is, suddenly all this drama is over. As long as you fantasize and keep dreaming about it otherwise, you deny the facts and the situation will keep you imprisoned in yourself. When you accept what is now, you will be free from it simultaneously.

As one businessman who lost all his fortune said: "What was I supposed to do - cry? Maybe ... for 5 minutes, and then get to work and rebuild everything." Do you know what happened to him? Now he is one of the richest people in the world, he lives next to the prime minister of his country, but do you know why? Because he did not go to pieces, did not give up, he fought even though it was a long journey, but he achieved success. As the biggest in business say that they went bankrupt several times, and lost all their assets several times, but now they laugh at it, because without it, without the moment when they had no bread, they wouldn't have achieved anything significant. The same is true for us. This advice may seem pointless to you at first, but after a long time, just like everywhere, you can see the effects. Everyone has difficulties, and everyone has a hard time, but no matter what happens to you, it's important what you do with it. No matter how many times you fall, it is important that you get up every time! Instead of developing new acquaintances, you waste your time on the elemental analysis of your ex's facial expressions and some kind of living in hope. The solution is (unfortunately) to let go of this woman and then try again with another woman. Give it up, it happened and that's it. I know this is easier said than done, but you have to let it go.

Flexibility - the readiness to change, the smooth transition from one state of mind to another. What will you do when a woman dumps you? It's easy: you will meet a new one!

DOUBT

"The best way to predict your future *is to create it."*

— Dr. *Joe Dispenza*

Nobody wants me, I will be alone for the rest of my life and I will not find anyone.

Is it rational?

- No.

Does what happened prevent you from meeting a new partner in the future?

- No.

If you lost your job, would you never find a new one?

- No

Are you lame or don't you have an arm and a leg? You don't have one eye? You have a hump like Quasimodo and you live in the basement? Come on!

There is a lid for each pot. She wasn't the girl for you. Work on yourself and move on and you'll be fine.

Who told you such things that you are hopeless or weak? Or maybe you let yourself convince yourself of this? You are a winner from birth, as a sperm you have beaten 200,000,000 competitors; it could have been someone else, maybe there was a doctor, maybe a lawyer, maybe a painter or a bishop, but you won! You were the best, the strongest, and the smartest of them all, but somewhere along the way, you got lost, you stopped believing in yourself, you ventured out physically and mentally. You are stuck in comfort. You need to remember who you are, find your real self. Get your balls back. Regain your power and strength! It's very simple, only a lot of guys who are still 'making a fuss on their ex' don't want to do it at all and keep making a sucker of themselves. It's time to end the mentality of the victim and pull yourself together. *You have to change.* You are not sure if she will ever get in touch again in her life. So assume she never will. The case is lost. However, the most important thing is to do something whatsoever. When you do something, it always reaps some fruit. You will finally reap what you sow. You go to a club a disco and you meet, someone who turns out to be your new friend. You go to the gym; you meet someone who helps you get a job. You run in the park and you meet an interesting girl. There can be many examples. Look at yourself from a distance, you have one life. I understand you, but do not waste the best years in your life, and you have a few more years ahead of you, pondering on the "woman" who, in addition, left you. There are so many things to do and see in this world and you want to lock yourself in one room with one girl. You're in an awesome moment to change your life 180 degrees. What do you get? Freedom! You can get a better, more attractive woman than your previous one and you can have a better relationship thanks to your experiences. You can kiss another one every night, and it won't be cheating. If she has someone else now. Be Happy. Now you have a free hand and you can try and screw whatever you want! *You can do everything, you are free!! You are the master of your life.*

Instead of contemplating on how beautiful it was and is no longer, it is better to think about looking for new unforgettable moments and that means new women. The road of a romantic, on which many doom themselves, is a suffering path to nowhere; it is knocking on long-locked gates, it is a waste of energy.

WILL THE SUFFERING EVER END?

"Those things that hurt, instruct."

– Benjamin Franklin

Many have gone through it. They feel rotten, emaciated, and crying one day they sniffed bullfinches on their sleeves, got up from their knees and, one by one, moved on with small steps. Man always comes out stronger in such situations. I got out of the shit so you will get out as well, because you are a guy and you have to be a behavioural model, not give up after the first major failure. Stand in front of the mirror and look at the guy you see who has done so many good things and can do 10 times more good. I don't fucking agree that some stupid bitch would destroy you. You are to pull yourself together and one day become a magical part of the life of a woman who deserves it and who will bear your children.

Everyone has had an unfulfilled love, but do you want to get stuck in place only to discover after many years that your life stopped at the point where you experienced the loss? Life is slipping away and there is a choice: if you live in the past and open up wounds, you stand still; and if you leave your sorrows behind and push forward, all within a decade you can have 5 unfulfilled loves, 17 love affairs and 2 fulfilled loves.

Some people need to fall to the very bottom, with such a big bang that it will still lie on the bottom. Sometimes people have to suffer even more before they wake up so that I can finally say, "I'm sick of this!" Only when you are fed up with your own illness can you free yourself from it, so it's about making a decision called "I'm done with this!"

PART 3

BEST VERSION OF YOURSELF

HOW MUCH YOU PUT INTO YOURSELF, YOU WILL GET OUT

You'll get out, what you put into yourself. And as much as you get out of yourself - a woman will know what a man you are. (A woman will know it intuitively by the body language, movements, behaviour, gesture, gaze, clothes, etc..)... So think about it- will the woman want to go running after you? If you are so cool, when it looks like you have seen many things, that you have found yourself in different situations and that you have found yourself in them that you can deal with it ... First you change, and then the world around will change. It will change itself.

I know no one here believes in a transformation that takes a few weeks. Neither do I. You have to develop the qualities of an attractive guy and they are key here, and they are not made overnight, but by hard work on yourself, which can take many weeks, months or even years. Work on reformatting your head before you completely get rid of jealousy, fear of loss, and develop the approach of "If that's her will, let her go."

At least half a year. I emphasize: half a year of intensive work on oneself and half a year of suffering pain for internal and external transformation. In the meantime, enjoy life by whatever it brings. Maximum, without any restrictions. You need to erase your ex out of your mind. Don't go to the gym for her, but for yourself. You just have to become a very happy guy.

You have to invest in yourself. So that you have something to talk about at meetings, on dates and not be boring, and you have to put a lot of stuff into yourself. Women a hundred times more prefer to hear from a satisfied, energetic man about his life once a week, than to sit subsequent evening of the week with lame duck whose topics for conversation end after a quarter of an hour. And why do they end? Well, what can you talk about when a "man" does nothing else, but waits from meeting to meeting and from text message to text message? There is only one way to the heart of a worthy woman: to become a worthy guy. There is no other way. Everything else is a theatre, a performance that always ends and ends in the same way, with more or less drama.

Answer the question *honestly*:

#1 If your daughter brought you in front of yourself, would you like to have such a son-in-law as you are at the moment? And would you like to someone like you to raise grandchildren with your daughter?

#2 If you were a woman and a guy like you would come to you, would you like to be with him?

If the answer is - No, why don't you do something to change it?

MAKE A ATTRACTIVE GUY OF YOURSELF

In extreme situations, gentlemen who are so immature, unprepared for relationships that, for the sake of the cause, they should immediately get out of their moaning relationships and spend a year or two on reconstructing or rebuilding themselves, and then look for happiness in love.

If a man does not start to develop, how is such a semi-intelligent, wimp going to create a *healthy* relationship with a woman? Since there are only fake dudes around, only 'colts', and 'puppets' who have nothing to offer a Woman! Women cheat, women are dishonorable, and women leave, etc. and I can honestly say that if I were a woman and had to deal with such guys, I would do the same too. Unfortunately, because the rest are smelly idiots who try to hide their own complexes and weaknesses behind a screen of artificiality and cunningness. If she couldn't cook, wash, clean, take care of the house, and became lazy, fat and do nothing with herself, would you still want to be with her? Likewise, you have the right to ditch a girl with whom a relationship would not give you the satisfaction you are entitled to expect.

So if women see the following in the street:

- admirers

- sidekicks

- loyal followers

- grovelling guys

- motherfuckers who use them

- those who can't even give them a substitute for an orgasm

So why should they struggle to get guys?

Are you going to pretend all your life to a woman as someone better than you really are? Do you want to cheat on her? Be yourself and work on yourself or else you will pretend to be someone you're not. And yet the essence of closeness and love is such that we can appear to someone without fear; naked and without armour on the soul.

Do you want to... DEVELOP?

Do you want to READ?

Do you WANT TO TRY, and to THINK?

Or do you prefer to find yourself an average girl, 'wet' your penis for two minutes, and ejaculate after 120 seconds? Yet, do you want to have balls though?

You have to be a *guy* with balls. If you aren't one, but just a namby-pamby, don't expect a nice woman. Everyone is selected according to their own esteem.

Do you want to raise your standards, and have *better women* who *will want* to get to know you, and *try* because she will see *something better* in you?

There are tons of very valuable girls in the world who are looking for a real man and most of them have already given up hope that it will ever happen! Be a real man, and stand up to the task, and you will attract women yourself. When a woman is 23+ years old, then she knows that there are loads of any kind of guy, and how hard it is to get a decent guy. Women *go crazy* after valuable men, and they shit in their thongs because of the fear of losing them. Even yesterday I talked about it with a friend, about the fact that her two closest friends are alone, because a valuable guy is a fucking scarce commodity.

> Make yourself a decent guy that the girl herself will want to meet!

YOUR ACTION PLAN

Your change! That is how have you changed?

Have you made the plan at all?

Was it studies, a car, an apartment, tennis, or models - or whatever you wanted achieve? Or you just keep doing nothing?

What plan did you choose for the time after the breakup?

For example, have you started playing the piano because you've always wanted to?

Will you, for example, learn to ski this winter because you intended to do so in the past, but there was never time?

Or maybe you learned to play tennis, but it is a difficult discipline, and the chick was taking up your time?

Or maybe you bought yourself a car?

Have you read an interesting travel book about Southeast Asia, where you are planning or dreaming of going?

Or have you learned Chinese, Spanish, or Russian?

What have you done?

What do you plan to do?

It's been time since you split up, so what have you done with your life?

Or maybe you are standing still and waiting!

For heaven's sake, wake up!

You are doing *nothing* with yourself.

Yeah, "I'll change my job after the new year". But what? What are you waiting for? For Santa Claus to appear?

After the New Year, now I don't have time, now I can't afford it …

Can't you afford sneakers and jogging in the park?

Can't you afford a blanket on the floor and 200 sit-ups a day?

Can't you afford to do push-ups at home?

Can't you afford to do squats?

Can't you afford triceps training?

No personal development, only the woman over and over again.

Studies, school, a better job, apartment, forester's lodge, car, bicycle, etc.

You come to work and what do you want to do?

"I would like to develop with you."

Do you understand?

Purpose.

Be specific. I want to be a lawyer, baker, or trombonist.

I want to complete studying at a gastronomic school, music school, or law faculty.

I like to fight, so I do MMA (Mixed Martial Arts), I like basketball and I like skiing.

Maybe you want to try snowboarding, golf or horse riding?

Do you understand? It's what you wanted.

Maybe model making? Or maybe go swimming? And perhaps forging horseshoes?

Do you understand?

Maybe to buy a new car, a new apartment, save money for your own flat; studies, roller skating, developing new skills, a dance course, a trip to India, running, gluing models, or painting. A long time has passed so what have you done with your life?

What have you already achieved? If it's nothing, then you are standing in the same place and falling more and more apart.

How many dates have you had since breaking up?

How many new women have you met?

How many have dragged you to bed?

Are there any long term plans? For example, buying a car, home, going on a sailing course? Are there any goals in life? Or is it just finding a woman??

If you are doing nothing, you must finally wake up! Stop waiting for her! Because you do not have to wait, but only *work on yourself* and *for yourself.*

EVERYTHING DEPENDS ON YOU

"We cry to God Almighty, how can we escape this agony? Fool, don't you have hands? Or could it be God forgot to give you a pair? Sit and pray your nose doesn't run! Or, rather just wipe your nose and stop seeking a scapegoat."

— *Epictetus, Discourses, 2.16.13.*

There is nothing worse than your own ineptitude and passive waiting for something to happen by itself. Nothing happens by itself. You think it would be better if everything came by itself, easily and effortlessly? The fact that we have to try, fight for what we deserve means that, in addition to the effort and pain that you have to put into your success, that *nothing* really depends on people *around* you. *Everything* depends only on *you* and on *how strong a guy you are*. Isn't that nice? Only from you. It is only up to you what you do with your life and not anybody and nothing else.

You can finally start living your own life and do the things you always wanted to do, but you lacked the strength, motivation and the balls to reach for them. You can do a massage course, enroll in a dance school (you do not need a partner, there are always more free women that you can meet by the way), you can do a parachute jump, bungee jump, get a motorbike licence, sign up for Krav Maga classes, start to leave the house, have a good time and meet women, and change your attitude towards people and life. Fulfilling your dreams gives you satisfaction with life. There can be many examples. Don't wait for a fairy-tale princess who will take your charm off you and change your life. Work on yourself, develop, act, try, search, build your world, and get to know yourself. When you are reasonably comfortable with yourself, someone interesting will appear naturally. Be like you feel good yourself, then the lady will appear herself and she will not be the only one, you will have a choice.

You have to work on yourself. So then?

Are you sure you are trying? Trying enough?

Maybe more effort is needed?

I went through it too, I suffered like a dog, and it was a nasty. One day a friend told me, "man, you will either have to get to grips with it, or tomorrow you will have to face a psychiatrist and drugs." Yes, I suffered so much by my misfortune that I almost fell into catatonia. All by MYSELF. This is the key word of all the fuss. Everything that happens in a relationship is a consequence of what you allow yourself and your lady. Everything that happens after the relationship is a consequence of what you allow *yourself* to do. As long as you think of it forever as a great loss, it will actually be a great loss and the end of life. Stop spinning because it's easier to drown in grief than to search for your own testicles with a pair of hands. You have to look at yourself in your own context. Fuck, are you worth nothing to waste months of your priceless, one-time life, because some girl abandoned you? If you're so weak that you can't tame yourself for fucking months - no wonder that the young miss has gone. She felt you were soft like a cheap Walmart pudding. So you fucking stop being soft. Among other things, so that no one can ever take another months of your beautiful life away from you again. The more valuable you are to yourself and the more self-sufficient you will be - the more precious and valuable you will be for every woman. The sooner you understand this, the faster you will recover. Understand this today, I advise you well.

Weak people are afraid to turn their heads away from the past and look forward, stretch their legs out from "was" and walk from "is" to "will be". That's why they cling to their ex's skirt, and that is why shaping the character is so important, because a strong character prevents:

1. Problems with yourself.

2. Problems in a relationship.

3. Complete loss of meaning in life after the breakup.

Act - this is the domain of Men. The boy in you must die because you're not going to be stuck in the past forever.

There is only one way out: ignore her, take a flashlight and look for your balls, in yourself and in your private life; don't look for them in a relationship, because you will not find them.

REBUILDING YOURSELF

Why wasn't I enough for her? Why did she stop loving me, what is wrong with me? We start to think about all our mistakes and shortcomings, about whom we are not and who we would like us to be, we screw up in our thoughts. This is an interesting process, because our self-esteem is already suffering. Do we have to hurt them even more? Would you say something ugly to your best friend? So why are you telling yourself this? The point is, do not feed on your own complexes with repeated beliefs in your head. Most people who have negative beliefs also have negative self-talk that creates a self-fulfilling prophecy. If this is you, STOP RIGHT NOW.

You have to believe in one person again, and that person is you. After 'failures', the most important thing is to rebuild yourself, your value. Believe in your worth again. You need to raise yourself mentally and you need to start building small successes now. It's all about those small successes. For starters (in addition to other activities) you can start running. The body moves, and you feel that you are a little better runner every day. You run a little further every day and you should strive to feel that you are starting to win again somewhere, anywhere. Even small wins count, that's why running is good, because you increase your route and keep running, but it could be anything else, whatever you want. Maybe you like running or swimming or cross fit, doing martial arts or lifting weights. Start winning. It is also very important to have goals in your exercise. Why? No matter what happened that day, you have something that went well. You ran further than usual, or you improved your time, or maybe you ran 3 laps more than the last time, you added a new weight in the gym. Do some sport. Another part of the brain directs the muscles, so if you really get involved, everything else goes away, your luggage is unloaded, and you feel relieved. There is only you and your body. Once you get involved, you don't think about anything else and it helps.

For now, you are probably still sending signals to those around you that you are unhappy, even if you don't realize it, because for now you are locked in a cage of sad beliefs about yourself. I guarantee you that it shows in you, in your facial expressions, in your body language, in how you behave in company and it is a kind of self-fulfilling prophecy. You feel that you are perceived as having little value, so you start to believe that your value is negligible and that you are perceived as such. When someone feels bad, uncomfortable with himself, he also affects people with whom he talks to or meets, or even just by looking at the person. This guy just "emits" tension and negative emotions, a negative atmosphere, feeling that he is not satisfied with who and what he is now. If you are unhappy, it's hard for a girl to be interested in your energy and who you are. Once you gain self-confidence, learn to swallow small failures easily, start to treat them as something normal, and they won't affect your self-esteem - then attack with all of yourself!

> High self-esteem is essential.

HIGH SELF-ESTEEM

"For when you cling, what you offer the other is not love but a chain by which both you and your beloved are bound. Love can only exist in freedom. The true lover seeks the good of his beloved which requires especially the liberation of the beloved from the lover."

- Anthony De Mello

Relationships of people who have problems with self-esteem, self-definition, clear definition of goals and needs, with their own limits, in other words - with dependent personality - are usually unsuccessful. The reason for failure is quite simple: such people enter a relationship with unrealistic expectations of the other person. Very often they try to get too close, beset and over-control them, they are full of jealousy, and get oxygen for life from their partner. We can safely say, the most important element of this life, because the relationship does not even know when it often becomes the most important area of life activity; and then imperceptibly from week to week, it's often the only area of this noble activity. The partner becomes a receiver-transmission station, which the dependent person must constantly send signals to and collect feedback from in order to define him or herself and confirm his or her value. An emotionally healthy, mature person does not allow him or herself to completely take over his or her life as a result of falling in love.

Work hard on yourself and your self-esteem, because you are very poor: you get addicted to her; you make yourself a reward from it and no matter what she is like "you can't live without her". Come on, man, re-evaluate yourself. I myself became convinced of my own worth. Do you have such a belief within yourself? If not, why the hell are you doing nothing to increase your worth? Self-esteem has to be high because this is the way to happiness. If you do not work on yourself, this weakness of yours will prevent you from having a lead relationship, sooner than later you will have failed miserably. Act on the basics, work on the foundation.

Work on how you feel about yourself. What are your beliefs about yourself? If these are clipping your wings, why don't you do something to change them?

7 Things you should do to recover faster

When your doctor diagnoses you, even if you expected it to be completely different, what do you do then? You accept it. You may not like it at all, but you follow the instructions because you know it's supposed to help you. Maybe the prescribed medicine is bloody bad, but the patient has to swallow it to recover. Maybe the therapy prescribed won't be the best, but you know it's for your own good, and if you don't, you won't get better.

1. Start training. Nothing works like the look of a guy who has physically changed. He started to have muscles, exercise his arms, lost 15 kg, or gained weight if he was too skinny, and this will also make you feel amazing about yourself. Exercise your body because this will give you confidence.

2. Renew neglected and valuable relationships. Perhaps you neglected your contacts with your friends during your relationship. Start going out with your friends and do fun things. Being around people who like you, love you, give you courage, and who you enjoy being with you is a great thing for mending a broken heart. Think about what you were doing when you were not in a relationship with her. You went out with your *friends*. Recconect with friends and family.

3. Go to the hairdresser for a fresh new hairstyle. Often, when we are in a relationship, we neglect ourselves and stop paying as much attention to our appearance as we should. We stop trying to look attractive. If you can afford it, go to a better, more expensive salon (check the reviews on the internet) and say that you want something new that fits your head shape and that you just look good in it. Later you can take a picture of your cut and show in a cheaper salon how you would like to have a haircut. If you have a beard, you can visit the barber or buy a beard trimmer. Hair must be well groomed, if you don't have hair, or your beard is very thin and patchy then shave smoothly. You also have to test hairdressers from time to time until you find the best one for you. Don't wait too long with trimming your hair (if it is short, then once every 3-4 weeks, if longer than 4-6 weeks).

4. Time for new clothes and improving your style. How they see you is how they perceive you. You throw away old things, there's no room for sentiment. Give back the old clothes, sell them or throw them away, but get rid of them. Don't keep the clothes you got from her if you strongly associate them with her, give them to someone, sell or throw them away.

5. Be more successful! This means that you find a job if you were unemployed before, or if you work in a corporation, climb up to a higher level. Maybe start a new career, invest in something. Just do something that will benefit you both professionally and financially.

6. Return to the passions that, by a strange coincidence, fell into a clinical coma. You had a passion, go back to it. You did not have a passion, find a new one.

7. Stop feeling sorry for yourself. Stop living with memories because new people, new experiences and new places are waiting ahead. Just give them a chance.

If you don't do these things, then don't complain about your life because you haven't really done the minimum to improve it. If you are not working on yourself, you are not trying to change anything, you know. Sorry, but no one will do it *for you*. The truth is that if you don't want to help yourself, no one will help you. It's not easy at all, but it's up to you to make the effort yourself. When it's bad, you can say to yourself: "bad days, you got me. Sorry to say this, but you don't stand a chance with me. I know it will get better and I want it to be better! I've already started working to make it better. I do these things to make it better, like... I take care of myself, exercise, meet new people, etc. that's why I can manage!".

IMPROVING YOUR APPEARANCE

Beauty is a relative issue. For one lady you will be on a scale of 6/10 and for some other you could be on a scale of 8/10. Added to this is the manner of being, self-confidence, posture, body language - it all adds up to how they perceive you.

- Take care of your teeth. It is quite important! It's embarrassing to be ashamed of your smile. Have you noticed how some people put their hands over their mouths when they laugh? They are ashamed of their teeth. Many women pay attention to a man's arms and hands, but also to details such as teeth when talking to someone. This can tell a lot about such a person, and it is not the best evidence of someone who has ugly, missing, neglected or broken teeth. Go to the dentist. Put on braces if necessary, get yourself implants, insert composite, whiten them, get any gaps filled in, treat them if any are sick, do everything necessary to make you feel better with your smile. This will add some very strong points to your attractiveness! What if it involves additional higher costs? Save money, sell unnecessary things online, do a second job during weekends. Is it worth it? Yes it is!

- Take care of your complexion and skin. Let's be honest. How you look matters. Her brain (a woman's) looks for signs of health in your body (health = attractiveness). If someone has skin problems, they don't look healthy. (Most often, the reason is processed foods and junk food). Your appearance also affects how you feel. If you need professional help in this area, take care of it.

- Appearance and hygiene. Basics: wash, bathe, use antiperspirant, shave your balls, shave your armpits and shave your virgin mustache; brush your teeth, get to grips with your hair, wear clean clothes, and iron them once in a while.

Take care of everything you can control and what you can't ignore.

- You have no influence on your height, but you can take care of your body.

- You have an influence on your clothes, and to keep them neat, clean and at their best (the best does not mean buying the most expensive clothes)

- You can take care of your complexion and your hygiene

- You can take care of your hair

Then stop completely worrying about your appearance. Pay attention to what you eat, exercise a little and accept your body as it is. I warn you against a maniacal approach to appearance, but you just have to take care of a certain level. Everything must go in the limit of compromise. If you do not want to take part in a competition, if you do not intend to devote every moment to training, it doesn't take much for you just to look good

PART 4

FINDING
REPLACEMENT
PART

It's the hair of the dog that bit you!

The truth is trivial because it is a cliché to say that time heals all wounds, and this is Gospel Truth. The Doctor of Time does however work better when helped by a nurse who looks at the wounded patient with tenderness. 'You have to change a little in order to choose well', can make the treatment process more enjoyable. It's the hair of the dog that bit you. There must also be an attitude inside that the 'new' must pass through an adequate amount of time. For one it will be one and a half months, half a year for another, and for yet another this could be a year, though only a NO CONTACT scenario can rescue you as well as trying out a new chick. Without it - you are still in the black hole at the back of your *ex*. When I started looking for another girl, I fully went for it, but I also picked up others, and this is the only way to free yourself from your *ex*. In time, you will think less and less about your ex, and it's very likely that in half a year you will even be laughing at yourself for your leanings towards your ex. Do your job, develop yourself and just be careful not to fall from the frying pan into the fire. Do everything in the right quantity, so there is time for learning, for dating, for developing yourself and for sport etc.

In one year's time you'll be laughing at yourself when you see a new woman at your side. In two years time you won't even remember what her tits looked like. After three years you'll be surprised by her very appearance, when you meet her on the street. Either she became ugly or she was never as beautiful as you thought.

How did the date with this other girl go? Tell me about this other one.

I am not interested in what she is doing now, who she goes out with or what her life is like - it is none of my business. My business is to find another woman in her place -> and that's where you have to redirect your focus, for a new you, rebuilding yourself and finding a new woman.

You've lost your woman, you've got an opportunity

Many people think that they will never get another chance in life and therefore focus only on the current situation. Such behavior is completely unreasonable, because, unfortunately, sooner or later it leads to an extremely frustrating situation when opportunity appears on the horizon.... and we are not able to use it, or worse still, even notice it!

Many guys go through breakup too much because they have started to focus on experiencing their suffering, not finding the 'replacement part' at some point. This behavior can be very dangerous because guys get depressed, start to go on the alcohol or neglect their work responsibilities, and it all boils down to the fact that they can't understand that a woman is a REPLACEMENT PART. Sometimes a guy experiences a breakup with a girl still 'with her in mind', but the situation changes radically when he meets another one who is similar in looks, though, a little prettier. In addition, she cares about him, and there is a good connection between them and he begins to do well with her. Love for the former one suddenly disappears; the cool character of the previous one also ceases to matter. He doesn't know the new one yet, but he feels happy meeting her. The reason you feel unhappy now is because you focus on what you don't have, what is beyond your reach, and what has become unattainable. Focus completely on the fact that there are many other attractive, suitable women around and the best times for you are yet to come!

Remind yourself of the two most attractive girls you've ever seen, but you've never talked to them or you've talked very little to them, and imagine that you would get one of them for a relationship, sex or anything you would like to have, but you would only get one of these two women and she would be chosen *randomly* by tossing a coin. How would you feel about this and how much would you care about which of these two women would become yours? To what extent would you think "GREAT!" I will get one of these two mega chicks, and no matter who I get, it will still be fine". You probably don't care about any particular woman; you want to have a woman with specific characteristics. That is, a woman as a provider of beauty, sex and emotional intimacy, bond and feelings. Would you like to go for a romantic walk holding hands along the beach, *randomly* chosen from these two women? Would you like to cuddle her tenderly or whisper how sweet she is? Hear *her* whispering that it is so sweet to be with you? Thinking about it, do you have the impression that in such situations you would feel deep satisfaction, not so much sexual as emotional? Don't you feel the emotional "twitching", as if you 'loved' this woman a little, you started to feel certain chemistry towards her, regardless of which woman among these two it would be?

A woman is a replaceable element - it's sad but true. Just realize that you are looking for *features*, primarily those of beauty, and not just a particular woman.

THE MYTH OF THE ONE IS A MYTH

Nobody tells you to pick up the *Queen* of England right away, start off with small steps. But damn it; go out somewhere, meet 5, 10, 15 women. You won't like every one of them, you will think about your ex even when you are with them - that's for sure, but don't give up, understand? Just *don't* give up! Because you will get one that will cure you! She will come like a bolt of light and before you know it, she will blow your mind, and your ex remains just a memory. You will be thinking about her for a long time, and then there will come a period of time in which you will think that you suck and nobody will want you anymore. But get over it, get through it and everything will be all right. Build yourself up, brick by brick. It will work out! It has to work out! You need to go out to them and become open and active, just like you did to your *ex* the first time round. She wasn't the love of your life then... but just another lady to pick up. And what was your attitude towards it? You've had your life.

Coming out of "the Matrix of relationship", such a guy realizes that he may have another woman, and he can also be in love and be happy! This is life, when you realize that every girl you have is unique to you, though not irreplaceable! You will not make your happiness dependent on external factors and her reactions. In time, you'll find that love can come back to you in the form of another person, that being a wonderful girl to fall in love with and to create a healthy relationship with. The longer you were with her, the more your recovery can take, but remember to be a man. You only get out of the swamp by working hard on yourself and for yourself. Now it remains for you to come up with a plan, roll up your sleeves, rub your hands together and get to work.

> In our time, everything can be replaced, you can be replaced, but you can get also someone to replace it.

How to meet a new and better one

Accept the fact that you won't pick up every girl you want. More girls will give you the elbow than date you, but it doesn't matter, because it's normal and none is irreplaceable. Accept success, accept failure, but also accept action. If it succeeds - great, if it doesn't work out - tough - the matter is out of the way anyway because we have some result. You did what you wanted to do. Accept that it may not work out; accept that it does not have to be perfect. You get the best effects with women when you don't care about the results. This attitude makes you more relaxed, and a laid-back person will always do better than a tense person. A chilled out man has more positive energy, and comes out better. Unfortunately, the *reverse* of this sentence is also true. Everyone turns out worse when tense and stressed, so don't worry about failure, only a fool does that. There are always ups and downs and thinking that every woman should react positively to you is ridiculous. Confidence will come when you see progress.

'Seek, and you will find' as it says in the Good Book.
You have to look.

I MET UP WITH ANOTHER WOMAN AND NOTHING CAME OF IT

"Today is difficult, tomorrow is much more difficult, the day after tomorrow is beautiful, but most people die tomorrow evening." - Jack Ma

It's not enough. You don't go out much to meet people. You don't know much about meeting new faces. When did you last meet someone? How many new folk have you met? You too rarely enter into relationships with the other sex. Go on a *date*, understand? I'm not necessarily talking about making love to a new woman right away, though... you should strive for it, or rather she should desire it. If you go on dates with five women a year, don't be surprised if you find the next woman in ... 10 years time. You do not appreciate the number of attempts that you just have to make to achieve some effect since we are guided by Disney fairy tales and film stories in trying to meet that one and only. He who seeks shall find. You need to dig some shells to find the pearl.

The only woman in your life that no one can replace is your mother. You will go out with another girl, and then maybe with someone else, because that's life... if you have the opportunity to meet others now, then do it... because it may turn out that the new one is better than the previous one, and even that is very likely.

Maybe, it simply takes time for you to meet a normal woman, doesn't it? Success with women is based on the same as success in business, sport, development and any other thing. You just have to act because it's always about getting yourself screwed up and picking yourself up again. You have to stumble 99 times to jump over an obstacle, you have to lose 99 times to win once, and sometimes you have to get through 99 weak women to find one awesome one and spend your life with her. You can't hurt yourself more than to close yourself to the world after a few bad experiences.

Give yourself inner permission and time to meet that new woman. If you always compare new partners to your ex, you'll never like any. In this way, nothing can please you. Explaining away things to yourself - as you will always come up with something means one woman will have thighs which are 3cm too thick, the other has crooked ears, and the fourth woman's nails are not so well varnished. The fifth will have a stupid friend, and the sixth a fluted heel that walks askew, the seventh will have a period, and so on, and so forth. I had to go through all those chicks that were not suitable before I specified those I definitely didn't want. These righteous, hardworking and good-for-life women also offer caring love.

It seems to you after a while that you can't feel something for someone else, that you can't stop loving the person who is in your thoughts. That's not true! Don't complain like most of you like "it's not the same anymore", because with a little perseverance, with the next girl you meet you will say "it's not the same, it's better!"

> Start dating other people. Don't necessarily believe the other half! Believe in thousands and millions of other halves! It works great on the mind.

IS IT POSSIBLE TO GET BACK YOUR EX?

There is fear, addiction, need and uncertainty mostly behind the desire to get your ex back. There is a lack of courage to get up and move on to the future. Going back to your ex is just taking the easy way out, and wasting so many great opportunities about. After long relationships lots of people have already forgotten what it's like to be alone and are terrified of it. We want to get back a woman because we are too lazy to achieve new goals! Our ego directs us! It dictates us to fix everything up.

Getting back to your ex turns out to be a good bet if two people actually match each other, are mature, and something connects them. And if not, then there is no chance for such a relationship to work out. I know cases of people who the ex-girlfriend came back to, but they all did something with one another like go to the gym, work, and develop, and change things for the better. The point is not to make such a comeback your primary, almost obsessive goal, rejecting in advance the possibility of a new relationship. It is unfortunately a very long way and not worth it, but everyone decides for themselves in their own understanding.

1. When you get back together with the woman you suddenly realize that it was not worth it and suddenly you remember that she is not so awesome at all.

2. Once you meet new women, there will be new enthrallment and you will be really surprised how quickly your desire to go back disappears.

Do you want to get back to her? Please do so, but it needs work and change. They see them, believe me. They will notice more in attitude than you are able to guess at all what has changed in other people. It is only the real power of contrast between what she knew and what is now i.e.- screwing her in the head like a club. Work on yourself, do not look for contact, and she will be surprised how you have changed. She parted with the wreckage of a man and is about to see the phoenix reborn from the ashes. For now, it's still the same and the girl has no reason to come back. You can stand still, and your woman has moved forward with her life, so who should she come back to if you don't suit her anymore?

How do you do it? It's simple - take care of yourself. Poor posture? Go to the gym; Overweight? Go on a diet; if it's puffiness in dealing with women - work on changing this. Such action towards getting back your ex truly only leads to getting yourself back. It's not about her. It never was. It's all about you. You would have to do the opposite of what your brain tells you to do in order to get her back. You would have to disappear from her life completely for a minimum of 6-12 months without any contact. The changes you make must be made for yourself and not for her. That is why contact must be completely cut off. Let her know it's over. And that's why there must be time for them to be convinced. There must be no contact with your ex and that's it, because when you break up, one text message after two months destroys everything. Breaking up and keeping out of touch means just that! How many people still do not understand the simple two words 'Break up', do not write, do not write back, and do not talk? You say you can't keep in touch, everything is clear: you say that you care but friendship is not an option, so thank her and say that you wish her the all the best. You turn around and go your separate ways. You don't write, don't call; when she writes, don't write back, when she's trying to get in touch, you say that you have explained to her that you are arranging a new life and you can't keep in touch. And so until she finally gives up. If she has the opportunity to observe you, somehow her potential curiosity is satisfied ...and it's easier for her to ignore you. If she loves you, she'll come back, but she's the one who has to come back and ask for your acceptance, not you. Since she broke up, she must strive to come back, and you must continuously work on yourself. She has to understand what she lost by breaking up with you.

Even if you get back together with your ex some time later she can walk all over you again and it will be the same as before, and this is not why you wanted to go back and do it all again, and to break up one more time in an instance. It's not about *showing yourself* to a woman after six months *as a more attractive guy*. The point is to really be like that.

A friend who parted with one woman had a:

New job, managerial position, own office, company car to his disposal. There's a new renovated cottage, money for an apartment stashed away and you know what turned out? He told me that he was actually doing what his 'ex' wanted.

Parting with another 'ex' that same friend said:

"Own job and company."

 "Developing new skills."

"University."

"New Home."

"Preparing for the purchase of a second, larger apartment."

"Roller blades."

"Overcame or got used to the fear of heights."

„He ran."

„He drives a car better."

"I behave differently towards women, without chasing after them."

"Preparing for the purchase of my own new car."

"Preparing, saving up for new furniture, according to my idea and taste."

"Preparing to go skiing."

"Everything and *everything* is mine!! My ideas and my desires,." - he said. The change that you are about to make is not meant to be for her or underneath her (you forget about her), it has to be only for yourself. You are to do it for yourself, and not for her to grasp her heart in a while. Otherwise it will not work.

But I'm afraid the better you get, the chick falls in your eyes. I looked at my ex after 3 years ....: Oh!? Now, she's a weak 3/10. The more you develop, the more you will see that you have more and more women. You will see! You will see that she is not as perfect as you thought. You will meet so many girls on the way that you will change your mind and even the best moments with *Miss Ex* will fade away. You will see. You may be shocked at how ugly and stupid a princess she is.

A guy who has strengthened his character, thanks to physically real work on his character, supported by deep self-reflection and strong motivation, will not be interested in changing and adjusting his ex-girlfriend to fit his new, stronger self. He won't be interested in playing, belching out her tests, and proving what a great guy he now is. Because being himself, he is able to build a lasting and stable relationship with a healthy, valuable new woman much faster. Only by gaining distance, recovering emotionally, gaining self-esteem, re-evaluating the system, he often sees that the previous set up was working badly. Healthier and wiser, they strive for a healthy relationship based on something different than before.

Until people change, it pulls them together in the same way and on the same basis as it did previously. For the same reasons, too, they are not suitable for each other as they were, and when they change or one of them changes, it will move forward - these people simply stop being interesting to each other. They are just looking for something else and someone else in life; someone else that suits them, and the former move on to a rarely opened album with old photos.

Men are able to work on their character, they are more likely to admit their mistakes to themselves, and it is easier for them to control their weaknesses. As for the woman, especially if she has brought along various problems from her family home, there is nothing to expect by any serious changes in her way of seeing the world and herself in this. An attempt to change the character and attitude of an adult who has this character shaped is doomed to failure, especially when it comes to women.

YOU, you, you, you, you!

And only you!

Sure of yourself!

Strong.

Ignoring things.

1. Do you want to get back? Then get back together, but on reasonable terms, without crying, begging, calling out like a perverted psychopath, sticking out on the estate, or on your knees. There are more and more desperate, would-be suiciders, and whining obsessors.

2. Breaking contact completely for half a year.

3. Breaking contact completely for 6 months.

4. Breaking contact completely for 24 weeks.

5. Breaking contact completely for 183 days.

Wait! Just 6 or *six* months. Wait! You will see that time will pays off. You'll get such a kick that it will be shocking. Be unavailable. The impatient always lose!

You don't care, don't show it. Remember – other girls also have it.

I once met my ex after 2 months after the breakup, and I got such a kick that I completely fell apart. I was recovering for a few days. If you want to experience something like that, and she has to see it, please, be free. It's an unearthly experience. After 3 months you delude yourself that you are ready, but the minimum is six months of intensive work on yourself and your life. Usually the situation is such that after these 3-4 months she continues to poison you. She writes to you, or you ask her for a meeting. She dates you out of boredom or for peace sake! Then we are not able to ward off emotions (bad advisers), we make a fool of ourselves again, and finally, you hit it all ON the SIDE, and you discover a heaven better, oh Seven Heavens better one.

The contrast. Did you do something for contrast? The power of contrast? Anything? clothes? Body? Other things?!

Getting back together is rare, mainly when people have been together for a long time, loved each other genuinely, but lost out to routine, and did not survive the crisis, etc. Then it is usually said that they needed a break to appreciate what they had. The remainder of getting back together follow the same pattern i.e. roads have diverged, but neither side has enough guts to embrace each other and close the chapter. Both are driven by sentiment and an anchor in the form of memories of shared moments that seem like a lost paradise. And then reality comes and the waking up quickly comes back to why 'it didn't work out'. Time was wasted, and it's back to square one, which is the day of the first parting.

Thinking about getting back together is hard work and not beneficial. They very rarely work out, because it is always like going through the same motions again. There is no way or any sense trying to rebuild your old values and place renewed relationship in this..... It will not work out, because it is something that has already happened and why the hell go back to it? Focus on building new relationships, that's it! Once they see your weakness, women will certainly not refuse to test your newly regained immunity and strength, at least from time to time - so do not be silly brother and do not provide her with more research materials in case of your breakdown. In addition, there are often issues related to the atmosphere in which the woman and the man parted. It is all the baggage that makes getting back together a very difficult thing, in a purely emotional sense, requiring a lot of strong and good will. If you believe it can be like it used to be, think about what 'in the past' really means, because , it will never be like it was at the beginning again. Ask yourself the question - do you really want you to get back together? It always takes time, willpower, and a lot of commitment. In my opinion, it's not worth it. But it is only up to you. Maybe she'll want to come back to you if you really do your best to get your house in order. But then you will definitely not want her anymore.

It is better to close this chapter

Advice in a nutshell:

1. First 'cure' yourself of your obsession with her return and stop analyzing every single thing about her behavior. Forget about anything without it.

2. Nothing will come out returning and, above all, from a new relationship without a firm resolution to change that which has faltered in you so far and to fall out of love with your own past.

3. WAIT. Patience for one is the flagship qualities of a real man. Self-control, emotional discipline, and inner self-control is essential. However, the real key to success is the power of contrast. CONTRAST. It's how much you've changed, and how many changes you've made. There's the gap between who you were and who you are now. This is in fact the only motive that is constantly repeated in all descriptions of getting back together.

Getting back together is like the sequel of movies, sometimes there are hits (e.g. Terminator 2) but unfortunately they usually end up as shit...

ONE DAY IT WILL ALL MAKE SENSE

"When one door of happiness closes, another opens; but often we look so long at the closed door that we do not see the one which has been opened for us."

- Hellen Keller.

My friend Robert had a fiancée, Laura. He planned a future together with her, a wedding date, children and family. Unfortunately, it so happened that his work colleague bangs his fiancée, which was a great misfortune for him. It was terrible to look at him, so the bitterness stayed with him. He loved her above all else as he himself said. More than a year passed by and he met a beautiful girl named Lisa. He was no longer moving on the ground but floating because he was so in love. Suddenly, however, also this time he was given the cold water treatment, when Lisa met someone else and decided to stay with that person. We were sad to look at him, especially the ruins left behind. He was dying of grief. Some time passed and Robert went abroad to work on a several-year contract. Imagine that he met a nice girl there who he married after some time. Currently, when several years have passed since that time, you can see that there is still a spark between them. Do you know what he thinks right now about previous broken relationships? He's grateful to those guys that they took those women off him, or else he would probably never have met his current wife. A longer perspective often shows that by losing something, you also gain something. Therefore, you should never assume that you have suffered a misfortune, because in this way we immediately record the event as a catastrophe and preserve the identity of the unlucky person and the victim, because not all losses are bad, there are also some that are blessings.

My friend Mark, who a few years ago, as a mature adult, good, grounded guy, made a special trip into the past and visited various places where he used to live. There, several times he managed to get in touch with various "princesses" for whom he was not a promising partner then for various reasons at that time. All these meetings were a shocking experience for him, showing that if then he had been 'successful' it would have been a serious life mistake. When he was much younger, he also happened to be ditched by women. He suffered a lot then, but as he says today he is grateful to them for it, because if they 'grit their teeth' as he says and agreed to what he was like then (quite serious deficiencies in various areas), he would never get to whom he is today. And today he is a happy man, very successful professionally, financially independent, at ease, and happy in the emotional and family scope. If any of these girls 'could have been with him all his life', he probably wouldn't have changed at all, because man is a lazy being and if something works, there is no need to change anything. It was the pain that forced him to start with a far-reaching programme of work on himself, where many of his weaknesses turned into their opposites. All these "catastrophes" were a happy twist of fate, giving a chance to achieve something more in life (including much better relationships and women). Unfortunately then it must have hurt – 'No pain, No gain.'

Often, after a few years, it can be concluded that any such loss or misfortune that happened to us was in fact a blessing under the mask of suffering ... but you only see it backwards, so long as you move on with your life, you do not give up, you work on yourself and draw conclusions. You have to experience certain things to become a new person, this better version of yourself, and life will give you exactly the experiences that you may not want, but need to get where you want to go. Life gives you these bad days so that you can begin to change. Life must have done this to you for your own good, because it knew that if you didn't push yourself, you wouldn't move it yourself. Maybe you say you want this woman, but the Universe or God says, "Wait a minute, wait. You have more options. She is not for you." "You won't get it because I have bigger plans for you. I see it better than you, there is more in you, and you have amazing potential. We'll get it out of you because I love you." And BOOM, the universe gives you a "problem" like a good parent says, "I know it hurts, I know you'll cry, it will be bad, it will be hard for you, but this is a stage, a process, and you will go through it. You have to go through with it. Everything will be alright." Instead of giving you what seems good to you and destroying you by it, he pushes you to something else that is better for you. You have to experience certain things to get the potential out of yourself. Ex is an example of what God doesn't want in my life.

Make sure that your life is on the right track and what is happening to you is as it should be - even if these are very difficult experiences to go through. What if the world turned out to be conspiring in your favour? Though, you will understand this only after many years. Everything has been provided to us for some purpose, even this painful experience has; this awful thing (as we look at it today) could have saved you from something much worse. Perhaps it will open you up to some amazing new opportunity that you are unable to comprehend right now. Why worry about it? We don't know what the future will bring. How do you know if your current girlfriend is the best, when maybe a few more are waiting for you? How can you be sure that the expectations you have today will not change? You have to realize that each failure and each success shapes us. The more defeats you get, the more you get to know yourself and your desires. Everything is as planned - remember that. Take from life everything that is given to you with gratitude and respect, because everything that happens in your life is a lesson that brings you closer to your great goal. Everything is going in your direction. Maybe it has to be like this for you to finally choose the one; maybe it has to be like this for you to learn how to deal with women. Perhaps it must be so, that we must learn from our mistakes. Maybe a little of everything. Do not feel sorry for your own fate, just get down to work, to hard work. In the end it will be okay, and if it is not okay it means that it is not the end yet.

None of us know the whole picture. We don't know what the rest of the story is and what it will be for.

THE END

Now take care of yourself and invest in your development and change, meaning both intellectual and external. Realize the fact that you are not just anyone, so find goals and pursue them. YOUR EX IS NO LONGER. Start living your own life, changing it for the better. Your ex doesn't exist for you right now, got it? She is out of your life - end of subject! One day you will thank her in your mind for it. Writing the chronicle of my battle, I must pay tribute to my 'love' ... because it was she who showed me, leaving me when I was weak, that as a man I was naked. She took the fake guy's coat off me. If your girlfriend dumped you, thank her. Rejoice as this may be the beginning of your victorious battle. Anytime and in any situation, you can rise to be stronger from being down and out. It is *never* too late for that. I am sure that you will find enough strength and patience to get up from your knees and be stronger and tougher, because you are enriched with the experience of loss. It's like men who carry their scars with pride. What you learned while collecting the whips on your own ass is only yours and that is why it carries undeniable value as any painful life experience with it. Later, not many things can break you. The hardest part is always at the beginning. Win against yourself. Know that everyone can be on top as long as they put a lot of work into it. Don't worry about the crap, go ahead and work on yourself, because this job is the best investment. It just pays better than any other business. In time, you will see a great, valuable woman and start a great, valuable relationship and family. Over time you will find out that love can come back to you in the form of another person. A normal, healthy, attractive and good girl you will fall in love with and whom others will envy you. You will love, and be loved again. Trust me! The longer you were with her, the more time your convalescence may take. But remember to be a man. Never give up! Don't let the temporary adversity grind you down. You only get out of the swamp by hard work on yourself and for yourself. The more valuable you are, the more that valuable women will be within your reach. Respect your friends and family as long as you have them, they are more important than a woman who can always leave, betray or even destroy you. Always remember that. Be above that and make your life fun and interesting especially for yourself, then a woman will only be a complement, and you can be happy with or without her. The dilemmas, failures, moments of breakdown happen to everyone, but persistence pays off and it pays off incredibly. You have to pick yourself up. Believe me it is possible. You just have to want it. In small steps. Do not feel sorry for your own fate, but get down to hard work. Give yourself time. Work on yourself. Love yourself. Don't look for a contact. Meet women. Endure. Cry. Keep training. Don't look for a contact. Work on yourself. Don't break down. Control yourself. Set goals and achieve them. Make perfecting, correcting what you don't want, what you don't like become your passion. Go your way, and let's never look back. Do not go back to the past. You accepted what you had to go through, because you know it was fair. What's more - you know you needed it. Be grateful that you could understand so much from it all. You got what you wanted. HER? NO! YOURSELF!!!

1. Change

2. Regain yourself and your strength

3. No contact

HAVE THE BALLS AND YOUR OWN LIFE

Take care my friend.

Leave a Review

Good luck, and do me a favor. If you enjoyed this book, I'd really appreciate it if you left your honest feedback. You can do so by clicking the link below. I love hearing from my readers and I personally read every single review.

http://www.amazon.com/gp/customer-reviews/write-a-review.html?asin=B09444Q89R

Printed in Great Britain
by Amazon

24025969R00118